The Price of Glory

Other Writings by Lillian DeWaters

All Things Are Yours ◆ The Atomic Age
The Christ Within ◆ The Finished Kingdom
Gems ◆ God Is All and Selected Writings
The Great Answer ◆ Greater Works
"I Am That I Am" ◆ In His Name
The Kingdom Within ◆ Light
Light of the Eternal ◆ Loving Your Problem
The Narrow Way ◆ The One
Our Sufficient Guide ◆ Private Lessons
The Science of Ascension
The Seamless Robe and Our Victory
The Time Is At Hand
The Voice of Revelation
Who Am I ◆ The Word Made Flesh

The Price of Glory

Dedicated to

The Spiritual Man—
"Christ in you, the hope of glory."

Lillian DeWaters

The Price of Glory

Mystics of the World First Edition 2018
Published by Mystics of the World, Eliot, Maine
ISBN-13: 9781946362230
ISBN-10: 1946362239

Cover graphics by Mary Pat Mahan
Printed by CreateSpace

DeWaters, Lillian: 1883–1964
Originally published: 1936
Lillian DeWaters Publications
Stamford, Connecticut

Contents

- Chapter I
  - Counting the Cost 7
- Chapter II
  - Entering the Path 14
- Chapter III
  - The Mediator 19
- Chapter IV
  - Christ or Jesus Christ? 26
- Chapter V
  - The Need of Rebirth 31
- Chapter VI
  - Who Is the Sleeper? 40
- Chapter VII
  - Individual Man 46
- Chapter VIII
  - Awake and Choose Ye 56
- Chapter IX
  - Ourselves and Others 68
- Chapter X
  - Healing in His Name 80
- Chapter XI
  - Practicing the Presence 92
- Chapter XII
  - Transcendent Love 104
- About the Author 113

"Believing in the One Mind alone, we make no attempt to change anyone or anything. The One Mind practices no healing. The One Mind gives no treatments. With Its own brightness, It *reveals* Its own perfection everywhere."

—Lillian DeWaters

Greater Works

Chapter I

Counting the Cost

Many today are seeking and praying for health, prosperity, happiness, and freedom, but few in comparison are aware of the price exacted for these spiritual blessings.

As in all dealings with material things, there is a price to be paid; so likewise in matters pertaining to the spiritual things of life, such as our health or our happiness of any kind, there is a price set for us to pay. So come now, and learn about the price of Glory.

Nothing but the failure to *recognize the truth about one's own perfect Being* and to *consciously live in harmony with it* has brought the terrible chaos which is on Earth today. And only as one pays this price—learns the truth about his own life as the perfect Son of God and learns how to think and live in conformity with it—will he begin to experience the heaven prepared for us all "from the foundation of the world."

We pay the price of our ignorance in suffering, in sorrow, despair, and lack. Surely an awful price to pay! But if we pay the price of Glory, the kingdom of heaven is ours.

"Awake thou that sleepest, and arise from the dead (the state of mental ignorance), and Christ shall give thee light" (Eph. 5:14). "In Christ shall all be made alive" (1 Cor. 15:22). "I can do all things through Christ which strengtheneth me" (Phil. 4:13).

Where is this Christ? He, the ever-living, all-loving perfect Christ, is here and now in you and in me! Not only as our ideal, our teacher, and wayshower, but He lives as our redeemer at the heart of our own true Being.

"Christ liveth in me" (Gal. 2:20). "Christ in you, the hope of glory" (Col. 1:27). "Christ is ... in all" (Col. 3:11).

Who, or what, is this Christ? He is often referred to as the inner Man, or the higher Self, and He is that in us who so often speaks the word of guidance, inspiration, or comfort, so that He has been called the "still small voice." The Christ in us is that which causes us to express the spiritual qualities of love, forgiveness, purity, mercy, meekness, and all that we call goodness.

But who of us has not recognized what seems to be two distinct natures within his own being? Often they seem to be in converse with each other—one, the weak, sinful, mortal man; the other, the wise, strong, spiritual Christ. These are the two of which Paul has so much to say in his various epistles, such as the following:

> I delight in the law of God after the inward man: but I see another law in my members ... bringing me into captivity to the law of sin (Rom. 7:22–23).
>
> They which are the children of the flesh, these are not the children of God (Rom. 9:8).
>
> For the flesh lusteth against the Spirit, and the Spirit against the flesh; and these are contrary the one to the other (Gal. 5:17).

Jesus taught us of "two men in the field" and "two women grinding corn," and "the one shall be taken, and the other left" (Matt. 24:41). Now, these "two" seem ever in conflict within us until we shall be born again—"born not of the flesh (ignorance) but of the Spirit (understanding)"; being willing to fully surrender "the old man with his deeds" and "put on," or accept, the spiritual Man with his spiritual activities.

Paul speaks both of the works of the mortal man and of the fruit of the spiritual Man, for he knew that through recognition of the Christ within us we become sensitive to His presence and thus consciously aware of the unworthiness of the personal life.

> Now the works of the flesh (mortal man) are manifest, which are these; Adultery, fornication, idolatry, hatred, envyings, and such like ... they which do such things shall not inherit the kingdom of God.
> But the fruit of the Spirit is love, joy, peace, long-suffering, gentleness, goodness, faith, temperance: against such there is no law (Gal. 5:19-23).

One's first effort in letting go the false man for the true should be to withdraw his faith and allegiance from those thoughts and things of the world in which he has hitherto placed them, and put all his trust in God and in the spiritually perfect ideas and things of divine Reality. Directing his heart and his mind more and more toward the fruit of the Spirit—such as love, peace, goodness, harmony, and perfection—one will naturally withdraw himself from the world and from its false creations.

The further one advances in insight the clearer and the more certain it becomes to him that *there must be a way*, other than the way called thought, whereby we can exchange our sorrows and problems for the true experience of peace and harmony. We feel intuitively that there is such a path—a living way of love and goodness. And there is. "I am the way," said Jesus, out of all bondage into eternal freedom. "I am the truth," replacing for sin and its workings the power of Love and Its fruitage. "I am the life," for I am he that redeemeth thee, and no man cometh unto the Father, but by me—by living, acting, being Me.

Suppose that you wish to move from the state of New York to the state of Florida. You would first have to make such a decision in your own mind, would you not? Suppose, similarly, that you wish to progress from the darkened mental state of ignorance into the true spiritual state of understanding. First of all, you are required to make up your mind and heart to the decision.

> For which of you, intending to build a tower, sitteth not down first, and counteth the cost, whether he have sufficient to finish it? (Luke 14:28).

There is always "the cost" to be paid in leaving the world behind, but the more certain and determined we are to take the required steps of spiritual transition the sooner shall we gain our inheritance of all good.

It is the *exchange of minds*—the giving up of the erring, unprofitable human mind for the unerring, illumined Christ-Mind—that will mark the hour of new birth for you. Can you decide to take this momentous step now and "let this (same) mind be in you which was also in Christ Jesus," or are you not yet fully persuaded that it can deliver you from "all the ills that flesh is heir to"?

Do you tremble before the *seemingly* mighty powers in this world, such as sin and sorrow, pain and poverty, or are you beginning to see that these evils are of the same nature as those which fell to the lot of the prodigal son, who wandered away from his father's house—evils which were, and are, *self-imposed*?

None of us, naturally, likes to confess that his troubles are his own responsibility—self-made and self-perpetuated. It is much simpler and less demanding upon ourselves to place the blame of circumstances on conditions outside and beyond our own control. But with the new birth comes the illumination and conviction that evil receives its power of continuance, as well as its origin, from man himself. The entity and power we give to evil by creating it and ignorantly serving it is the only entity and power that it need have for us.

If we would "put on the Lord Jesus Christ," then we must pay his price! We must learn how to look upon evil in the way that Jesus did. In fact, to follow Jesus in all things is our only sure way out of the darkness of ignorance into the understanding which is Light.

Through his own spirit of Truth, Jesus healed the evil called sickness and cancelled the unclean spirit called sin. He used only spiritual means to transcend the human self and set people free from sin and ignorance. Moreover, he taught that all these had their beginning within the man himself, for he said:

> There is nothing from without a man, that entering into him can defile him: but the things which come out of him, those are they that defile the man ... For from within, out of the heart of men, proceed evil thoughts, adulteries ... thefts, covetousness, wickedness, deceit, lasciviousness ... blasphemy, pride, foolishness: All these evils come from within, and defile the man (Mark. 7:15, 21–23).

Let us not, therefore, foolishly try to rid the world of evil by applying our efforts directly to world conditions, but rather let us change the complications to be seen in our world by *changing man himself.* Verily, the world to be found outside him is first of all in man's own heart and mind; therefore, change your world by exchanging your personal mind and heart for the mind and the heart of the one "altogether lovely," Jesus Christ. In what other way could one really expect to change a world?

Now, we may not be able, all at once, to serve the Christ-Mind only, but we can surely make a beginning, and every time we think and do the things of love, of peace-making, of honesty, faith, purity, and goodness of any kind identified with the heavenly order, we are using the mind of Christ.

As we earnestly and lovingly work to change our world conditions by first bringing about the necessary change *in ourselves*, we shall be paying the price of Glory; and here and now in this, the prophesied "fulness of time," we may hear Love's benediction: "Come, ye blessed of my Father, inherit the kingdom prepared for you from the foundation of the world"—the kingdom which is the effect of righteousness.

How many of you who read this book are willing now to resolve to give up your personal self, and all of its inverted activities, in order that the mind of the Christ may be expressed in you and in all of your associations and affairs? To many of you, this will indeed be a difficult task to undertake, but when the habit has been established, it grows to be a *natural* way of deliverance, bringing a sweet sense of peace and security immeasurably well worth the price of all personal surrender.

How many of you who read this book would be willing to ask some reliable and unbiased friend to tell you just what he sees in you which is not measuring up to the Christ way of living and acting? Could you listen unresistingly and without self-justification, should someone lovingly point out that fault in your disposition which impedes your spiritual progress and which might act as a stumbling block to another?

A higher way, even, is to relive each day as the impersonal onlooker. "Did I permit myself to be influenced or overpowered by some selfish thought or feeling?" Ask the Christ in you to answer. This exercise will enable you to increasingly live each day as the real Self and will sharpen your judgment as to what is really true or false in your relation to the day's events or to your personal contacts.

Unless you are willing to do this in order to develop spiritual insight and higher living, you ought not to murmur when chastening comes upon you for the omissions and the commissions of the life you are leading.

> God dealeth with you as with sons; for what son is he whom the father chasteneth not? But if ye be without chastisement, whereof all are partakers, then are ye bastards, and not sons (Heb. 12:7-8).
>
> The Lord your God proveth you, to know whether ye love the Lord your God with all your heart and with all your soul (Deut. 13:3).

Every day makes higher demands upon us, causing us to increase our spiritual vision and our active embodiment of the one and only Power, God; the one and only Man, Christ in you; and the one and only world, the kingdom of heaven, at hand.

> No man, having put his hand to the plough, and looking back, is fit for the kingdom of God (Luke 9:62).

Chapter II

Entering the Path

No one need feel that he is too deeply mired in sin or in trouble of any kind to be unworthy of the ever-ready help and the everlasting love of God. He need only be willing to receive the truth about his own Being, then leave all to conform to it, that he may become "a new creature in Christ Jesus."

To "put off the old man with his deeds," as Paul says, is part of the necessary price demanded of each aspiring soul entering the path of Glory. Man's troubles have come to him only because he has served the wrong master, the mind of the world, or because he is trying to serve two at the same time; trying to give a hand to each, though they are going in opposite directions—one, the "wisdom of this world," and the other, "the mind which was in Christ Jesus."

Yes, verily to be free from the oppressive fear of evil of every kind, as well as from all the painful limitations and restrictions of this world, we must receive our spiritual Selfhood and let go the mortal part of ourselves, and of others, which has led us so far astray. As we come to accept, to love, and to serve the perfect Christ-Self only, as the one Reality of all that is, we naturally more and more desire to turn from sin of all kinds and separate ourselves from it.

Becoming consciously at one with the true qualities of our real nature, such as love, meekness, mercy, righteousness, and forgiveness, and manifesting a full and undivided faith in God and His Christ as the *one* reality of us all, we will find that our troublesome disorders of mind and body, together with all bondage and limitation, will fade away of themselves in the same way that light must negate darkness.

So the mortal man whom you have accepted yourself to be—the sick, limited, and sinful personality—is to be "put off," and you are to "put ye on the Lord Jesus Christ," the real Self of you, always perfect and ever one with the Father, for "that which is born of the flesh is flesh; and that which is born of the Spirit is spirit" (John 3:6). And verily, when you seek these blessings—true health, true wealth, and true happiness, which are of spiritual origin at their source—you will find them.

Our *real* Identity is never that of mortal man, for he is but the erring expression of that individual who does not know or embody the truth of himself. The real Identity of each of us is to be found and claimed in the one infinite Christ Selfhood. As we substantiate this Reality of ourselves, we will gradually leave behind us the earthbound states of suffering and limitation induced by self-will, self-love, self-righteousness, self-justification, self-pity, and all the unlovely traits which characterize the unawakened soul.

The true inner Being of us all, the Reality of each one of us, is the one tender, radiant, and "altogether lovely" Jesus Christ Selfhood. So meditate upon this perfection of yourself often until this spiritual fact has taken firm root in your consciousness, and moreover, earnestly strive to express the Christ qualities in your home and in your association with the outer world; for it is only as we identify ourselves with Jesus' way of thinking and living that we are empowered to bring into our lives the freedom which he promised us when he said:

And ye shall know the truth (about all things), and the truth (realized and lived) shall make you free (John 8:32).

For example, once, in speaking with a man about the Jesus Christ Selfhood abiding in every breast, he confided to me his difficulty in loving a particular relative who he thought had wronged him many years before. He realized the great importance of always manifesting love and forgiveness, and for a long time he had been trying earnestly to force himself to love this person, but without any success. When it was shown him that he need not strive to love the mortal parts of this individual—the part which he had been seeing as so faulty—but instead he could freely and fully love the Christ in him, the true Self of that man, he saw this great freeing truth for the first time, and something in him leaped for joy.

Simultaneously, as he felt this burden which he had been carrying for years slip away, he saw how natural, how easy, how beautiful it is to love the Christ of a person rather than the mortal appearance of him. And not only was he freed, then and there, from the confusion in his consciousness, but perfect harmony was very soon restored between these two, and a breach closed which had long separated them. Moreover, at the same time he experienced an instantaneous physical healing. He was automatically set free from an ailment which had troubled him all those years and which had persisted despite all his treatment for relief—material, mental, and spiritual.

Some form of sin is often the cause of physical illness or limitation, yet the particular fault or the specific mental cause may lie unknown to the sufferer for some length of time until he, or someone else, is able to set him right with God in his own heart and life. Jesus alluded to this law of spiritual unfoldment when, after healing one diseased for thirty-eight years, he said unto him: "Sin no more, lest a worse thing come unto thee" (John 5:14).

Again, there are those who, when told of their mistakes, persist in remaining blind to them, refusing to accept the loving admonition given by others in their behalf, bringing forward instead arguments and reasons in self-justification. In such cases these people may not be healed of their troubles until they have made a full *surrender* of their personal will and have learned to live in *obedience* to God's will for them.

"If we say that we have no sin, we deceive ourselves, and the truth is not in us. If we confess our sins, he is faithful and just to forgive us our sins, and to cleanse us from all unrighteousness" (1 John 1:8-9). We all learn, sooner or later, that sin brings inevitable suffering. But such suffering is spiritually educational; otherwise, there would be no law of justice operating in a world predestined to come into the knowledge of the truth.

When one learns the awful price he pays for sin, how much more willing he is to abandon it for the higher life! Really, it is not only the right thing to do, but more helpful in every way, to *rise out of* painful mortal experiences through our vision of man as the perfect Son of God and through our willing *embodiment* of him in our thoughts and actions, than it is for us to try to overcome the evil conditions of our world by combating them with material and mental means. In fact, a mere intellectual acquiescence to good thoughts, without our loving embodiment of them, will but help to make us cold, egotistical creatures indeed.

Why should anyone expect to experience perfect health, harmony, happiness, and the abundance of all good here in the flesh unless he be willing to fulfill the divine requirement, which is that he shall *manifest perfect love, righteousness, purity, and honesty, and ever place his faith in God as all-powerful and thus all-sufficient to meet his every material and physical need.*

Perfect Love was the paramount quality which Jesus expressed and revealed as the true nature of us all. He exemplified pure and boundless love toward God and man, embracing all in forgiveness, mercy, loving-kindness, tolerance, and compassion.

If, however, instead of expressing the altogether lovely qualities of our Christ-nature, we express the opposite of them and try to make our way in this world through selfishness, egotism, unforgiveness, hardness of heart, and sharpness of speech, we are fortunate indeed if any trial, no matter how painful, brings us face-to-face with the consequences of our sinfulness so that we can renounce it completely and express instead only the true qualities of purity, love, and goodness. Surely this is but a small price to pay for the happiness we are seeking.

Chapter III

The Mediator

Do not limit the birth of Jesus, the Christ, to the historical event of two thousand years ago, but open wide your *spiritual* vision and see that the birth of Jesus in the lowly stable typifies how he, the indwelling Christ, appears in the life of each individual right here on this Earth today.

Verily, "unto us (each) a child is born." In studying the story of the birth of Jesus, we find that he was born of Mary, a virgin. So in trying to gain a true knowledge of this event in ourselves, we discern that the first spiritual requirement is that we shall have a virgin consciousness made up of purity and love. How could we expect to invite the presence of the perfect Christ if we are entertaining a consciousness mixed with selfishness, pride, and impurity?

Where the "manger" of the heart is prepared, there will this heavenly Child be born. When we are eager to make ready in our hearts a place for this "express image of his person," then soon shall we find him abiding with us. But the Holy Child cannot be born in him whose mind is in a state of selfish ambition or desires of the personality, but only in him who is lowly of heart and of a spirit of meekness and self-effacement.

None may set the hour when this Child shall be born in us or when we shall awaken to a knowledge of His presence with us, but when we have made ready the place, lo, soon we feel Him with us. Then the Herod-mind of the world will seek to locate and destroy Him. The sharp comments and adverse opinions of others not yet awake to the revelation of this new life would distract our attention if we listen to them, so that we must "arise, and take the young child into Egypt"—into the secret place of silence and protection.

Be still. Tell no man. The bird broods quietly upon her eggs. The seed rests in the earth in stillness, undisturbed. So also should we let the Christ-Child abide in us in quietude and confidence, or until we are certain that we are ready to let "the government" of all our earthly experience rest "upon his shoulders."

We know not how the egg is absorbed by the birdling, nor the seed into the plant. So with our individual spiritual awakening, we know not the exact hour when we shall "awake in his likeness" or when we shall be delivered from our sickness, lack, and trouble. But as surely as the wise men came to hail and worship the Holy Child, so will true experiences come to glorify the event of His birth in our consciousness.

Today when we ask, "Master, where dwellest thou?" we hear the ineffably tender answer: "Behold, I stand at the door and knock: if any man hear my voice, and open the door, I will come in to him" (Rev. 3:20). Only by first closing the door of his thought against the claims of personality and materiality does one prepare his consciousness to later admit the Christ who is his genuine and true Being.

We cannot behold the radiance of our perfect Christ, nor share in it, when we give our attention only to the things of this world. Our great concern should therefore be to learn how to become at one with this "Prince of Peace" within us, who is ever our life, love, truth, joy, peace, harmony, and the abundance of all our good, continually and everlastingly.

We may have already contacted this inner "hidden man of the heart" by the use of texts and books about him and through preachers, teachers, and churches, as well as through our own prayers and spiritual revelations. Many of us have through these means touched the hem of His garment and received divine light and great good; but problems have still continued to perplex us, darkness has again overtaken us, and often we have questioned if there be any end to this journey in pursuit of our complete happiness. However, as we continue to use these means to press on, we arrive at the perfect answer, the one complete and all-satisfying answer, which is "Christ in you, the hope of glory."

> Who is the image of the invisible God, the firstborn of every creature (Col. 1:15).
> That was the true Light, which lighteth every man that cometh into the world (John 1:9).
> The Father loveth the Son, and hath given all things into his hand (John 3:35).

It is asked, "How can we come to that high place in consciousness where we may become at one with this indwelling Presence of light and power?" First, by closing that door in us which leads to confidence in, and dependence on, the human or personal self; for so long as we try to overcome "the world, the flesh, and the devil" by efforts based upon our own human mentality, just so long shall we be occupied with a procedure which is not only fruitless but which delays our spiritual awakening. Second, by embodying the nature and very Being of the Christ-Man. Verily, to surrender the false sense of personality and to put on the true understanding of Jesus Christ will surely be the means of delivering us from evil and unifying us with our true Being—the spiritual Christ-Man; for did not Jesus himself say, "Whosoever will lose his life for my sake shall find it" (Matt. 16:25)?

When we see that the name *Jesus*, as given to the Christ-Child, is the real name of us all, we shall begin to understand why it is that we can be saved only in His name.

> I bow my knees unto the Father of our Lord Jesus Christ, of whom the whole family in heaven and earth is named (Eph. 3:14-15).

It is because Jesus Christ, "the only begotten Son," is the family name for us all that he is the *mediator* between ourselves and God. "There is ... one mediator between God and men, the man Christ Jesus" (1 Tim. 2:5). Who but the man Christ Jesus, always recognizing himself as one with the Father, ever said, "Follow me"? Men since the beginning of time have pointed to other great persons as saviors, but Jesus pointed to himself, saying boldly, "Follow me."

The man Christ Jesus represents Spirit in action, Spirit in feeling and in form, announcing, "He that followeth (after) me shall not walk in darkness, but shall have the light of life" (John 8:12). He taught that when he appeared to men in human form, they should raise their vision of him to that of the *manifested* Christ—"Emmanuel, or God with us." Did he not say to the mystified Philip, "Have I been so long time with you, and yet hast thou not known me, Philip? He that hath seen me hath seen the Father; and how sayest thou then, Show us the Father?" (John 14:9). None but the man Christ Jesus said, "Ye believe in God (the Father), believe also in me"— God in form to human sense and sight; God in action, in loving, living expression.

Furthermore, he said, "Without me ye can do nothing." Without our acceptance of the Jesus Christ Man as our inherent perfection right where we stand, we cannot be saved from the evil of this world, for it is written, "I can of mine own (personal) self do nothing." Furthermore, no man ever lived on this Earth who spoke of himself as the savior of all mankind but Jesus Christ. He said, "No man cometh unto the Father, but by me" (John 14:6). "He that believeth on me, though he were dead, yet shall he live" (John 11:25). Though he were weak in both mind and body, though he were poor in all this world's goods, and though he were unhappy and lonely without friends in this world, still, all that he longs for or his heart could desire is already fulfilled in the one Jesus Christ, his very Self and Being, and his only way back to the kingdom.

Over and over again, the question is asked, "What does it mean in the Bible when it says that we can be saved only through Jesus Christ—that he alone is our redeemer, savior, way, resurrection, and our full, complete, and only salvation"? The answer can only be understood spiritually; that is, by one who is sufficiently purified of personality to receive and accept it.

Raising our consciousness from the belief of Jesus as a human being to the spiritual perception of Jesus as the Christ, we perceive that he is the divinity and the reality of each of us; hence his name is the family name for us all. How could we ever hope to be saved from sin and delivered from the "far country" of mortality in any way other than by knowing *who* we are—knowing the name of our true identity?

Can you, for instance, rightfully lay claim to any material possession today by using any name except your own? Then why should you expect to lay claim to your *spiritual* inheritance of perfection and life everlasting by using any name except the name of your own true identity, which is *Jesus Christ*? Thus, by embodying him as our divinity and identity, we shall awake in his likeness "and be like him ... filled with all the fullness of God."

Now, there is a marvelous and matchless way of deliverance described to us so beautifully by John, the beloved disciple of Jesus, in the following words: "(God) loved us and sent his Son to be the propitiation for our sins ... and not for ours only, but also for the sins of the whole world." The natural question now is: how can Jesus Christ, the Son, be the propitiation, the cancellation and absolute forgiveness of our sins today? In this way: through our individual acceptance and embodiment of him as our genuine Identity, our original and ever existent perfect Being.

In proportion as we "put on," or accept and receive our true estate of Sonship, are we set free from the thinking daydream of sin and its consequences. Insofar as we permit it to be our divine Selfhood, the perfect Jesus Christ will be the propitiation for our sins, here and now.

To illustrate this: you can readily see that your full and free deliverance from the sleeping dream is vested in you yourself in proportion as you remain awake. Therefore, you, the man awake, are the propitiation for all the dream errors you commit in your sleep; for as soon as you function in your waking state, then all the mistakes of your dream are lost sight of—are they not?

Applying this dream illustration to our daytime experience, which includes the thinking-dreams of sin, sickness, and limitation of all kinds, we can readily see that in proportion as we receive Jesus Christ as our very Self do we experience our *full* and *free* deliverance from all thinking-evils; for he is the "free gift" to man and the propitiation for all our sins and for the sins of the whole world. Unifying ourselves with him rather than operating in the separate human personality, our deliverance is certain and assured. He, our real Identity, gives for our (personal) sins, His purity; for our (personal) ignorance, His understanding; for our (personal) weakness and shame, His power and glory.

Paul tells us plainly: "By grace are ye saved ... and that not of yourselves: it is the gift of God." The dictionary gives the definition of grace as follows: "Grace is the state of reconciliation to God through Jesus Christ." In order, therefore, for us to be saved by grace, the free gift, we must of necessity "put ye on the Lord Jesus Christ," for it is certain that we cannot as personal human beings ever be one with God.

In proportion as we *embody* our real Being, our Lord-Self, we are automatically and effortlessly set free from the sins of our human state. Thus, our only hope of complete salvation through Jesus Christ is for us to *rise in consciousness, hence in experience*, out of the corruptible mortal state into the incorruptible immortal state.

Now, as grace is the unmerited love and favor of God in Jesus Christ, the price of Glory is paid as we accept of this free gift. "The gift by grace ... is by one man, Jesus Christ" (Rom. 5:15). It remains for us only to accept it, then to present and explain it to others, even as Peter stated, "As every man hath received the gift, even so minister the same one to another" (1Peter 4:10).

If now in our consciousness we resolve to give up the age-long belief that we are human beings—in consequence subject to sin and its punishment, lack and its limitation, sickness and its retribution—and instead be intuitively ready and willing to *be* and consciously *manifest* our original spiritual nature and Being as ever one with God, we may share, here and now, in the vicarious atonement; for Jesus Christ, our real Identity, will freely blot out all our sins and cancel all our suffering. Verily, one's own true Being brought forth into *individualized* power and action does now, as at all times, set him free from the law of evil.

Chapter IV

Christ or Jesus Christ?

We read in Genesis that God created man in His own likeness. Who was this man? And where is this man now? Does it not seem reasonable that if you knew his name and identity it would clear away the mystery surrounding the text? The time has come now for you to hear and clearly understand the truth about this spiritually created Man.

We have here set before us *two* men—first, the Man made in God's image and likeness, and second, the man made out of sleep and dust. We are plainly told that the name of the second man is Adam, but the name of the first Man is left for the individual's own spiritual discernment. However, the New Testament writers have given it to us, and they use the names *Jesus*, *Christ*, *Jesus Christ*, and *Christ Jesus* interchangeably. There was never any doubt in their minds but that Jesus was the Christ and the Christ was Jesus, and no matter which name they used, they referred to one and the same Being—*the Man made in the image and likeness of God.*

The disciples had raised their vision of Jesus' human form to that of the *manifested* Christ; they saw the man Jesus as the *express* image of God. For Peter, when questioned, significantly answered, "Thou art the Christ, the Son of the living God." And Thomas, also discerning this truth, said, "My Lord, and my God."

Only as we see that Jesus Christ is the firstborn of us all and that it is He who is our real nature here and now, can we be permanently delivered from the sin, disease, and death which characterize the personal, or Adam, man. "For as in Adam all die, even so in Christ shall all be made alive" (1 Cor. 15:22).

Since Christianity is founded upon Jesus Christ, it is imperative that we should have a right and clear understanding of him, and also a right and clear understanding of our identification with him, if we are to establish our lives on the "Rock which is Christ" and bring forth the fruits of righteousness, peace, happiness, and harmony. Jesus was divinely sent into this world to express to humanity the fullness and the completeness of the Man made in God's image and likeness—the Man who is the identity of us all and verily the "firstborn of every creature."

> God ... hath in these last days spoken unto us by his Son ... the express image of his person (Heb. 1:1-3) ... The image of the invisible God ... For in him dwelleth all the fulness of the Godhead bodily. And ye are complete in him (Col. 1:15; 2:9-10)).

Throughout the ages prior to the advent of Jesus on Earth, the Christ, God's spiritual idea of Man, had been expressed to a greater or lesser degree in the lives of prophets and saints, but Jesus was the only one of whom it is written: "God sent his only begotten Son into the world, that we might live through him" (1 John 4:9). Jesus was therefore not only a great example and a great master but he was infinitely more: "Emmanuel, which being interpreted is, God with us" (Matt. 1:23). Spiritually understood, Jesus was "God manifest in the flesh" to show humanity its divine nature.

> God was manifest in the flesh. (1 Tim. 3:16). Christ Jesus, who, being in the form of God ... was made in the likeness of men (Phil. 2:6-7).

Now, what does the wonderful name *Jesus* signify? What is its spiritual interpretation? This name means *savior*: "For he shall save his people from their sins" (Matt. 1:21). The man Jesus personified the savior-Christ: he, the "firstborn" of each of us, is the savior of us all.

> God ... hath ... given him a name which is above every name: that at the name of Jesus every knee should bow, of things in heaven, and things in earth, and things under the earth; and that every tongue should confess that Jesus Christ is Lord, to the glory of God the Father (Phil. 2:9-11).

As our bodily organs were all conceived, or created, in the mind of God before there were any of them in visible manifestation (See Psalm 139:16), so Jesus, the savior-Christ, abode in the mind of God *from the very beginning.*

> Jesus Christ the same yesterday, and today, and for ever (Heb. 13:8).
> God ... called us ... not according to our works, but according to his own purpose and grace, which was given us in Christ Jesus before the world began (2 Tim. 1:9).

To think of Jesus only historically, that is, as a man who at that time through the Christ of himself overcame mortal conditions, deprives one of the inspiring and unifying understanding that the spirit of Jesus Christ is here and now in every creature! "Know ye not ... that Jesus Christ is in you?" asks the awakened Paul. Also: "For ye are all one in Christ Jesus" (Gal. 3:28). For those who can accept that the *Christ* is within them but cannot see or accept that *Jesus Christ* is within them, let it be seen that this obstruction in their consciousness is caused by their thinking of Jesus as the human concept of man instead of understanding him as God's spiritual idea in manifested form. Verily, verily, it is written: "Who is a liar but he that denieth that Jesus is the Christ?" (1 John 2:22). "Whosoever believeth that Jesus is the Christ is born of God" (1 John 5:1).

Now, we know that things of the Spirit can only be spiritually discerned and understood, even as Paul declares: "The natural man receiveth not the things of the Spirit of God: for they are foolishness unto him: neither can he know them, because they are spiritually discerned" (1 Cor. 2:14). No one, of course, could accept the statement that Jesus as a physical being is within us, but when one intuitively perceives the spiritual truth about Jesus, he then translates his concept of him as that of a human personality into that of the manifested Son of God. Then he can easily see that this *spiritual Identity* is the one only begotten Son of God and is essentially in each and every one of us.

In speaking of our unity with him, Jesus said:

> At that day (of your individual spiritual awakening) ye shall know that I am in my Father, and ye in me, and I in you (John 14:20).
> As the branch cannot bear fruit of itself, except it abide in the vine; no more can ye, except ye abide in me (John 15:4).
> That they all may be one; as thou, Father, art in me, and I in thee, that they also may be one in us (John 17:21).

Thinking only abstractly of the Christ has kept humanity from the higher realization that *in every one of us* abides this same Jesus Christ perfection. Thus, when the Christ-idea was presented to the world in the visible, tangible form of Jesus—the very personification of divine Good, absolute purity, life, truth, and love—the awakened soul of man then saw, felt, and knew that the invisible Christ-idea and the visible Christ Jesus were one and inseparable. Verily Jesus showed forth to sight and sense the perfect Man who is ever-present and within us all, becoming visible to us to the extent that we experience him.

It was the disciple John who in his Gospel spoke of the great love of God toward the whole world in the following verse: "For God so loved the world, that he gave his only begotten Son, that whosoever believeth in him should not perish, but have everlasting life." Then let us open wide our hearts and minds that we may be able to truly believe in him and spiritually comprehend that the universal Jesus Christ is the *individual* perfection of us all right where we stand.

This living, ever-present Christ in us must be glorified, and only as we call upon Him, love and trust Him utterly, can He glorify Himself in us and through us be the expresser of absolute Love—loving thoughtfulness, kindness, peace, joy, harmony, affection, and all the fine and noble qualities which inhere in his Being.

Yes, the individual must so put off the "old man with his deeds" that he will thereby become a pure transparency to reflect the radiance and the glory of the risen Christ.

> Therefore if any man be in Christ (be reborn), he is a new creature: old things are passed away; behold, all things are become new (2 Cor. 5:17).

Chapter V

The Need of Rebirth

In the thought of vast throngs of people on Earth today, is it not the limited mortal self whom they recognize and consider almost entirely? Our newspapers tell us minutely all about this man. They narrate in detail the limitations and destructions which surround him, the accidents which befall him, and the punishments which overtake him. Yet we are advised in the Bible to cease thinking about man from this viewpoint and with this short perspective. Why? Because it is the false viewpoint, and "if the light that is in thee be darkness, how great is that darkness." Truly, if one's only understanding of God's creation is that of the mortal man in a material world, how great is such darkness!

Let us face some of the problems troubling humanity today. Never before in human history have men of every nation struggled more intensely to keep from slowly sinking into the depths of failure and despair. Governments are undergoing the strain of the inner and outer conflict despite heroic efforts to save or explain themselves, and one who is spiritually awake cannot fail to see the inadequacy of the mind processes of man to govern himself and his world successfully and harmoniously.

We see, for instance, the failure of man-made laws to banish crime from the Earth and the ineffectiveness of scientific education to eliminate sickness, accidents, and death. Paradoxically, the breaking of man-made laws but increases his need for more laws; the failure of his methods of material healing but accentuates his necessity for more hospitals, institutions, and cemeteries. And so, hither and yon, ever flickers the great searchlight sent out by humanity in its vain effort to find its peace and harmony, its holiness and real happiness here on Earth.

Without ever waking to the hopelessness of the personal man and his shortsighted methods to ever bring about the permanent effects he seeks, the great mass of people desperately continue the search to acquire these in the "far country," where "no man giveth unto him." Verily, the depravities and vanities of man's own imaginations must first "be burned as with fire," for it is not God but *man* who has created a world of disease and hospitals, sins and prisons, death and cemeteries. How obviously true is the statement "God hath made man upright; but they have sought out many inventions" (Eccles. 7:29).

Never has humanity stood in greater need of a knowledge of the truth which will bring to it the real salvation than right now. The heartbreaking struggle for freedom, for peace, for happiness and plenty will come to an end only when man lays down his sense of the personal life and takes up the "cross," which is its cancellation and negation. Then will he rise in consciousness to embody in his daily living the Christ-Self "which lighteth every man that cometh into the world."

Said Jesus, who knew all things, "Ye must be born again." This is a spiritual demand which none may escape. Rebirth is that baptism by the Spirit which neutralizes the waywardness of the mortal heart and mind, reorienting the individual to newness of life—to new hopes, new ideas, and new affections. This new birth, the surrender of mortality for the acceptance of our immortality, reveals the Sun of Righteousness which "arises with healing in His wings," dissolving the clouds of darkness hitherto surrounding man.

Dear reader, are *you* ready to give up the dream of mortal existence—which is sometimes a nightmare, with its griefs, pains, and at best its impermanent joy shadowed by fears—to become "a new creature" in Christ Jesus? If so, then "cease ye from man, whose breath is in his nostrils: for wherein is he to be accounted of?" (Isa. 2:22). Reverse yourself! Cease striving for the "added things" unlawfully. Crucify the selfish personality.

Have not many of us been trying hitherto to put off the *deeds* of the "old man," overlooking the fact that it is the old man himself who is the root cause of all the evil deeds? Paul states it clearly when he says, "Put off the old man with his deeds," and Jesus likewise said, "Now the axe is laid unto the root of the tree (the remedy is applied to the consciousness of man)." Therefore, instead of directing our attention toward the *fruits* of evil, such as pain, sorrow, and despair, we should raise ourselves into the Christ-Consciousness which *makes such conditions impossible.*

If a tree in an orchard is allowed to grow, fruit is likely to appear; but if the tree is cut down at its root, fruitage is rendered impossible. Therefore, if we wish to remove the liability to sin, be sick, or be in lack, we must apply our whole attention toward cutting off these mortal conditions by *surrendering the personal mind and self* for the Christ-Mind and the Christ-Self. Then, and then only, have we laid the axe unto the root of the tree.

There must be a cancellation of the man of sin, not only from our thinking but from our behavior as well. Unless these two—true thinking and its experience in true living—go along together simultaneously, a man will remain spiritually barren until his vision opens more fully to the divine requirement of his *complete self-surrender.*

Speaking of the mortal self which must be relinquished for the Divine, Isaiah tells us: "But we are all as an unclean thing, and all our righteousnesses are as filthy rags; and we do fade as a leaf; and our iniquities, like the wind, have taken us away" (Isa. 64:6). We find Paul, too, speaking in no uncertain language about this mortal man state which is to be surrendered, for he says, "Let God be true, but every (mortal) man a liar" (Rom. 4:2).

So dear one, if you are restless and troubled mentally or sick and disturbed physically, look deeply now into your own consciousness and try to discover if there be any weakness, shortcoming, or selfishness there; if so, resolve to give it up, and the darkness cannot long perplex you with the coming in of the light. Thus, as you increasingly unify your thoughts and actions with the perfect Christ-Self, turning away more and more from the old ways of personal thinking and living, the dark cloud of fear, lack, and all pain and suffering will vanish from your everyday experience.

It may seem to be the most difficult and preposterous thing in the world for us at times to say, "Not my will but thine be done," yet there come occasions in our lives when nothing short of this absolute surrender of the personal self will deliver us from our troubles. And blessed are we when we can lay down not only our will of what is obviously wrong thinking and acting, but more than this, when we are ready to give up that which our personal will considers justifiable and best for us in the case, according to the earthly standards, and let our Christ-Self alone outline and guide.

> If therefore the light (one's personal opinions or prejudice) that is in thee be darkness (not God's will for you), how great is that darkness (how greatly do you need to practice meekness, self-surrender!) (Matt. 6:23).

On the other hand, it sometimes happens that when we earnestly desired a certain thing to take place in our life, we later see that it was not best for us that our prayer be answered in the way we wished. God, our true Being, is always nearer to us and all our affairs than we can ever believe, and as we learn how to think and live in harmony with God's plan for us, we shall find this Earth a very wonderful place in which to live—verily, heaven itself.

The Gospel reads: "For this corruptible must put on incorruption, and this mortal must put on immortality" (1 Cor. 15:53). *Where* and *when* may such translation take place? What better place than here and now? This verse is not to be applied to that common incident called "death," as though the passing of a man from one level of consciousness to another could automatically and magically deliver him from sin to glory, from ignorance to understanding, and from corruption to incorruption. No—a thousand times no! For *now* is the day of salvation, not that hour when you leave this world through death and are lost to the sight of those still here. *Now, while you are still present among us on Earth, this is the hour for you and for all mankind to be reborn*—to give up the temporal and self-imposed state called mortality by renouncing and turning from it, and "put on the Lord Jesus Christ" by embodying fully and completely your only Being as the image and likeness of God.

Man then becomes a new creature, not by dying but by turning from the mortal to the immortal of his own Self and Being. "There is neither Jew nor Greek, there is neither bond nor free, there is neither male nor female: for ye are all one in Christ Jesus" (Gal. 3:28). The question for your decision is: am I looking to Christ Jesus as an example who died long ago, or am I looking to Christ Jesus as the one Immortal of us all—omnipotent and omnipresent here and now?

Truly, there can be no continuous and noticeable spiritual progress in our everyday living, no steady growth in grace or any permanent achievement without the miracle of rebirth through self-surrender and our acceptance of the one spiritual Man as the one Immortal of us all.

The idea back of the word *self-surrender* is of the greatest significance, and we do not hear this word spoken of or come in contact with its deep meaning often enough in the religious instruction of today. It should be considered the prerequisite of all religious experience, for all must come to see and value its transcendent importance in the life of everyone.

Let us ask and answer a question which perplexes many a student of truth today. It is this: why is rebirth through self-surrender a spiritual prerequisite in order to partake of our divine perfection, when we have heard it preached that man is *now* the Son of God and is *already* God's perfect image and likeness? How is it that if I am made in God's likeness, hence innately perfect, I am required to fulfill all the conditions of rebirth out of the life of the flesh into the life of the Spirit?

We would point out in answer to this question that the Bible teaching never implies that as human beings we are perfect now in this earthly experience, nor that we are *consciously* at one with the perfect, indwelling Christ until we have, in full cooperation, *accepted and embodied* Him. It is the Christ-Self of us, the Reality back of every personality, which is perfect now, and although this perfect Man is our essential Being right where we stand, nevertheless we must experience Him inwardly and express Him outwardly if we are to manifest our perfect estate "on earth as it is in heaven."

Therefore, as one accepts the actuality of the Christ-Man as the real Being of all mankind, and as he comprehends the *impotence* and *unreality* of the mortal man state, he will surely bring the spiritual good of his real Being into his everyday living. In repeated parables, Jesus reiterated that the kingdom of heaven is worth every sacrifice—*even to the unconditional abandonment of the personal self*! How beautifully and practically he stated it:

> Except a corn of wheat fall into the ground and die, it abideth alone: but if it die, it bringeth forth much fruit (John 12:24).

The gospel of *self-surrender* is therefore the gospel of living and doing. By his own example, Jesus showed us what there is for each of us to do before we can experience the fulness of our perfect state; and did he not give us commandments such as the following, which we are to obey here and now?

> Thou shalt love the Lord thy God with all thy heart, and with all thy soul ... and with all thy mind. And (thou shalt love) thy neighbor as thyself (Luke 10:27). Ye must be born again (John 3:7).

Thus, daily practicing the surrender of the faulty mortal man for the perfect spiritual identification, we shall withdraw our interest proportionately from the limited human dream state until we have become completely at one with the indwelling Christ, who alone has dominion over all. "All power is given unto me in heaven and in earth" (Matt. 28:18).

To perceive through spiritual intuition—the only way that we can perceive it—that our true Being is the one "only begotten Son of God," and to hold steadfastly to this realization in thought, deed, and action, will ever be sufficient to deliver us from all our problems in this field of experience on the Earth-plane. The divine requirement asks no less of us than this difficult "way of the cross" of cancellation as the way to give up our human personality. This means that we *surrender* our personal will, our personal self-righteousness, self-justification, self-defense, self-love, self-condemnation, self-conceit, and all that selfishness which goes with the personal man.

"He that humbleth himself shall be exalted," announced Jesus. When, through our love and devotion to God and His spiritual requirement of us, we are willing to give up our sinful, selfish thoughts and actions and humble ourselves before God and man, so that we may express that Son in whom He is "well-pleased," this humility on our part receives the instant recognition of the Father within, and His blessing is expressed in us through our spiritual exaltation and our recognition of another victory over the personal man. For the promise reads:

> Humble yourselves in the sight of the Lord, and he shall lift you up (Jas. 4:10).

Verily, the man who has become a prodigal must humble himself, repent, and seek restitution if he would escape being humbled by God; for it is certain that if we do not obey the spiritual command—"Humble thyself"—then He must needs discipline us. Few, if any of us, escape the divine chastening which, though often painful and discouraging, is fruitful in the end, even as Paul says:

> Now no chastening for the present seemeth joyous, but grievous: nevertheless afterward it yieldeth the peaceable fruit of righteousness unto them which are exercised thereby (Heb. 12:11).

We will all be able more and more to throw off the errors of the personality as there is rooted more firmly in our consciousness the conviction that there is that Self within us which is truly "the image and likeness" of our Creator, and which must ever be triumphant and "o'er all victorious." Hearken now to this voice of your Christ-Self as He speaks intimately to you:

>Peace I leave with you, my peace I give unto you (John 14:27).
>
>If ye abide in me, and my words abide in you, ye shall ask what ye will, and it shall be done unto you. Herein is my Father glorified, that ye bear much fruit; so shall ye be my disciples ... If ye keep my commandments, ye shall abide in my love ... Love one another, as I have loved you ... Ye have not chosen me, but I have chosen you ... that ye should go and bring forth fruit, and that your fruit should remain (John 15:7-8, 10, 12, 16).
>
>The Father himself loveth you, because ye have loved me, and have believed that I came out from God ... Be of good cheer; I have overcome the world (John 16:27, 33).

Chapter VI

Who Is the Sleeper?

When we are asleep at night, there is that of us which is greater than the dream—which can end it because it is no part of it. Note these three points carefully until you can grasp and accept them: there is that of us which cannot be harmed by any man or beast we may see in the dream; which cannot be hurt should we seem to be falling from some great height, nor injured by fires, storms, or dangers of any kind whatsoever; and if we would turn in consciousness to ourselves in our comfortable room, the dream, together with all its alarming pictures, would dissolve.

In the same manner, while we are *spiritually* asleep in our daytime experience, ignorantly thinking and feeling sickness, sorrow, lack, or any kind of trouble whatsoever, there is that of us which is greater than the *thinking-dream*, which can end it because it is no part of it. Immersed in our troubles, our dangers, and our problems, if we would but turn to the perfect Christ-Self of us, the Self which is ever-present and *always* at hand—beyond and above all harm, transcending all thought of hurt or destruction of any kind—if we would but trust this Self and more than all else desire to become at one with this Self, we would soon begin to experience relief from the distressing situations of our everyday living.

Suppose that in your night dream you seem to be participating in some sinful course of action and you wish for a way of escape from its consequences. There is always this sure way open for your perfect vindication, is there not? Just to *awaken* and come back to your normal state of awareness on the bed!

As soon as you are awake in your room, you are automatically delivered, not only from the punishment you feared in your dream, but more than this, you can now see that the sinful state or condition never really took place at all, for the water, the land, the people, the circumstances, and the conditions which one sees and feels in a dream are but unreal inventions or imaginations of the man who is dreaming them, are they not?

In the same manner, man can deliver himself today from the evils which he fears in the thinking, daytime dream of sickness or of any kind of trouble, by an *awakening* which takes place in his consciousness when he learns to discriminate the real Self and the real conditions from the unreal self and the unreal conditions. As he withdraws himself from the false position of "sleep"—the mental state of thinking and acting which is contrary to the perfect and immaculate mind of the Christ—and claims his oneness with God through Christ Jesus, his spiritual Identity, he will be able to experience, to sight and sense, emancipation from the distressing thinking-dream and deliverance from its seeming discordant conditions.

It can easily be seen that when one functions in his normal waking state he is automatically cut off from the sleeping dream. Likewise with the individual who functions in his true Christ estate; he too is *automatically* cut off from the discordant thinking-dream of mortal experience, for all that permits the picturization of his earthly troubles is for man to wander in thought and action from the true Being.

It was in the parable of the sower that Jesus said, "But while men slept, his enemy came and sowed tares ... and went his way." While men sleep in *forgetfulness* of their real Christ-nature and of their continuous perfection in Him, these hallucinations are sown in their minds, and the tares of discordant mortal conditions, such as poverty, sickness, and trouble of all kinds, spring up in their experience.

It seems to be quite generally believed that it is the mortal man who is the sleeper, or dreamer, but it should be seen that mortal man is *the man in the dream* of material existence and not the dreamer of it.

To discriminate between the mortal man who is the man in the dream and the dreamer, we need only turn back to the common experience in sleep and see that the discordant man you think you are in your dream is not the man you really are on the bed. Therefore, it is the man in the dream who typifies the mortal man of our daytime experience, for it is he who is showing forth the chimerical appearance of sickness, limitation, and the many other shortcomings.

Naturally the next question which arises is this: *who* or *what* is the cause of the mortal, discordant man? Have you not many times thought deeply about his appearance and wondered who was responsible for it? Suppose, for illustration, that you stepped into a room where a man lay asleep, and having the power to look into his dream, you see that he seems to be out in a blizzard, struggling with wind and drifting snow. You know at once that this man in the blizzard is not a true or a real man, but that he is caused, or produced, by the man who is *asleep*.

Whom, then, does this man on the bed (the sleeper) typify in our waking experience? It is certain that he must be the one who is responsible for the appearance called the "mortal man" as well as for the mortal conditions of sin, sickness, and all the multitudinous forms of limitation on Earth today.

Although the answer to this momentous, all-inspiring question can be plainly stated in a few sentences, nevertheless it requires deep insight and spiritual intuition on the part of the reader to *receive* it. "When the disciple is ready the master appears"—so may all who have earnestly desired to be told the answer to this question, and are ready to hear it, be immeasurably blessed and benefited hereby.

Each one of us is an individual soul, or consciousness (illustrated by the man on the bed), and we fluctuate between our essential spiritual Being (the man awake) and the mortal man of our material existence (the man in the dream). Inherently we are not the mortal man; he is but the out-picturing of our ignorance and forgetfulness—that mental state which Jesus called "sleep." Although the spiritual Christ-Man of us is essentially our only Being, still we do not experience this estate of perfection here on Earth except as we "put on" and embody Him in our *thoughts, words, and actions.* Therefore, the sleeper is none else than each individual soul who does not remain *awake* and *aware* of his *inherent changeless perfection.*

We all stand in an *intermediate* position, as it were, between the perfect spiritual state of us and the imperfect mortal state of us. Thus, the admonition is given: "Choose you this day whom ye will serve" (Josh. 24:15). The man on the bed dreams unconsciously until he is able to understand how to control his dreaming. So likewise in this world, it is the mortal, or personal man, whom we each *unconsciously* show forth until we learn in Truth how to rise out of the mortal state of consciousness into the Divine, and thus gain dominion over that state of mind which Jesus called sleep.

Understand, dear ones, that it is never the Christ, or the spiritual Man, who dreams or mistakes his way. The Christ-Man is ever awake and is always one with the

Father since he is Life, Truth, and Love in manifestation. To this end were we created, and toward this goal must we ever progress, that we may know, love, feel, and be this living, ever-perfect Christ-Being who is, individually, all of us and, universally, one indivisible whole. "Be ye therefore perfect" is the divine dictum.

If, then, we keep awake, consciously aware of our ever-present Reality, by steadfastly facing our inherent, changeless perfection as the Man made in God's image and likeness and by conforming our daily living to the divine principles of love, purity, and righteousness, there will be created for us, right where we stand, new life, new strength, new flesh and bones, or whatever the physical need seems to be, for the eternal promise is:

> Behold, I create new heavens and a new earth: and the former (things) shall not be remembered, nor come into mind ... And they shall build houses, and inhabit them; and they shall plant vineyards, and eat the fruit of them.
> And it shall come to pass that before they call, I will answer; and while they are yet speaking, I will hear (Isa. 65:17-24).

The appearance of a human being in the midst of sin, sickness, or poverty is not the *true* representation, or the reality, of that man; for there is always that of him, unrevealed and obscure to the outer senses, which is his Life, his Spirit, and his genuine Being. When one can recognize this truth about himself and lay down his false sense of life, he may declare, right where he stands:

> I am the perfect Son of God! I am one with God in all things! All power is given unto Me!

Even though he may appear in the midst of poverty, the depths of sin, or the throes of suffering, if he will claim this truth, in faith and with his whole heart, soul, and being at one with it, holding steadfastly to it with the complete dedication of his attention, the super-imposed dream-belief will fade from his mind, and simultaneously the evil or discordant condition will disappear from his experience. He will then enjoy emancipation and know to a fuller degree his original and ever-existent estate as the Son of the living God.

Chapter VII

Individual Man

Let us turn to the story of the raising of Lazarus as given to us by St. John. We read that Jesus came to the cave in which lay the body of his friend and that great sorrow and weeping prevailed among the people gathered about the place.

After approaching the cave, Jesus must, first of all, have turned within himself to the Father—his own ever-perfect state of Life, Truth, and Love—for he said, "Father, I thank thee that thou hast heard me, and I know that thou hearest me always." Then, realizing sufficiently his oneness with this infinite Spirit of all, he commanded in a loud voice, "Lazarus, come forth."

Many of us may have pondered in our minds over the question as to whether Jesus addressed himself to the spiritual Lazarus or to the mortal Lazarus. That is, to whom did Jesus call loudly? Truly this is a cardinal point to consider and a searching question to ask ourselves.

If one answers that it was the spiritual Man to whom Jesus called, then he is assuming that it was the spiritual Man who was asleep; for it must be remembered that Jesus spoke of this condition as that of sleep, inasmuch as talking with his disciples about the sickness and death of Lazarus, he had said to them, "Our friend Lazarus sleepeth; but I go that I may awake him out of sleep." Now, how could the spiritual part of Lazarus, the reality of him, verily the Christ of him, be asleep, even in that prolonged sleep called death? We know that this could not be possible, for the indwelling Christ is an ever-living, never-changing Christ, "the same yesterday, and today, and for ever."

On the other hand, how could Jesus have addressed the mortal man, when it is written that "in Adam all die"? How could he have called to the material or personal man to come forth into life and action, when he himself had taught that "the flesh profiteth nothing"? Of course he could not, and he did not. The average student and thinker has considered but two factors in this case: one, the spiritual, real Lazarus, and the other, the mortal material Lazarus. But with a wider and a fuller understanding of Life and Being, one sees that Jesus could not have addressed either the spiritual, perfect Man or the false, personal man.

Then who is the "Lazarus" to whom he called? For many years the author sought and prayed that the answer to this mooted question might be revealed to her, which answer, of course, is involved in the previously considered question: who is the sleeper? The answer finally came as a revelation—that is, it came directly from God, or the Christ within.

Although it appears that we must consider man either as a mortal or a spiritual being, according to the two generally accepted categories of man, there is, however, a vision which over-arches and transcends this belief. In this higher vision, we see that man is *primarily* an individual soul, or consciousness, and from this starting point he can act either as one with his essential Christ-Being or in acquiescence to that state which is called mortal existence. We all stand in the *middle ground*, or neutral place, as it were, between these two states—that of our original pristine Perfection and that of the assumptional mortal man.

Lazarus, as an individual soul, or consciousness, had evidently allowed himself to believe in and accept the mortal state of sickness and death. Jesus, with transcendent vision and sovereign power, cried with a loud voice, "Lazarus, come forth!" Inasmuch as a sleeping consciousness can always be aroused into its natural waking state by one who has the sufficient understanding of Life, Jesus commanded Lazarus to awaken from his sleep, and instantly "he that was dead came forth."

In order to understand more clearly how one can be awakened from his thinking-dream of sickness or any kind of lack or limitation, let us turn back again to the illustration of the man on the bed, dreaming that he is out in a blizzard, and let us see how we would stop this man's dream and do away with all the distressing conditions in it.

Of course you would not appeal to the man in the blizzard, for you would know that the man on the bed is the only one responsible for the whole thing. Intuitively you understand that this man on the bed may express an entirely different aspect from that when asleep, that is, when he is *awake*; moreover, you know that in yourself you have the power to turn him from his state of sleep back into his waking state just by calling to him.

You do not call to the man in the blizzard, nor do you call to the man in a waking state, but you turn to the man asleep on the bed, and calling him by name, you waken him. Then all the conditions of his natural state are restored to him, and the dream, with all its chimerical pictures, vanishes.

Wishing to apply this vision, luminous with the light of divine Truth, to those discordant conditions appearing in one's everyday experience, we turn back to the instance when Jesus came to the grave of Lazarus. We now see clearly just what the dream situation portrayed. Lying in the cave was a dead body, "bound hand and foot with graveclothes: and his face was bound about with a napkin." Standing about were many weeping relatives and friends, all sad and hopeless. This is a picture of mortality, for it is all opposed to the *im*mortal man and his *im*mortal realities.

Now, just as one would not call to the dream-man in the blizzard nor to the man awake, but to the sleeper, so in like manner Jesus did not call to the dead body nor to the spiritual Man, but to the *sleeping soul back of that body*—the consciousness responsible for this very dream.

You have seen in the illustration of the night dream that back of every dream-man there is a sleeper who can be awakened; so in the same way, back of every mortal-appearing man, there is a *sleeping consciousness* which, if willing, can be awakened and so restored to his natural state.

What will help one to awaken and advance more rapidly in his progress toward a more harmonious existence? Direct guidance from God. How can this be accomplished? First, by having the simple faith in God as a child has in his earthly father. Second, by feeling a deep, heart-filled love for God as his Creator and the supreme Force and Power in his life. Third, by laying the problem before Him and expectantly waiting for the answer.

The most important part of prayer is for the seeker to receive a *direct answer from God* concerning it. An illuminating feeling may come over him, a feeling of uplift and exaltation which means to him that "all is well." He may hear specific words of directions, or there may be only an inner feeling of conviction regarding the certain step to be taken. If one practices contacting God this way and receives the answer, he will find the greatest blessing of his whole life, for he will always be led along the right path, and delays and mistakes in the working out of his problems will be avoided.

Indeed, this simple method of direct guidance is the most beautiful thing in one's life. It is the great Fountain, always open and ready to quench one's thirst; it is the all-loving Presence embracing one in the simple assurance that "I will never fail you nor forsake you."

The author could relate hundreds of occasions where she has received direct guidance from God relating to particular problems. This guidance has very frequently come as distinct words or a simple sentence which would *immediately* right the condition. Again, the direction has come as a feeling of exaltation, or an intuitive understanding, and many times she has received her perfect answer by opening the Bible at random, but with all-absorbing devotion and expectancy. The answer would lie directly before her vision—and this answer has never failed. The closer we live to God the clearer will be our vision and the swifter and surer our contact with God.

Only Truth is successful. Therefore, the more of Truth you embody the more successful you will become. Let him who is faced with limitation on any side or concerning any achievement, whether health, happiness, or prosperity, *cast out of his life every action unlike divine Love*. Let him deeply, earnestly, and all-absorbingly *feel* his love for God, and feel also that there is no inner withholding of love from any person on Earth. Divine Love in oneself will illuminate any cloud of darkness and swiftly dissolve the seeming problem. Love, and *love alone*, is the never-failing solution to all our problems.

When advanced in consciousness to spiritual Being, man will not appear as a separate personality but as a distinct, individualized consciousness, embodying the identity and divinity of the one "altogether lovely,"

Jesus Christ. Not our personality but our *individuality* will forever be retained.

If we wish to experience and demonstrate the glory and power of God in our lives today and manifest here our true understanding of Being, we must not only translate our sense of the personality of Jesus into the spiritual reality of him, but moreover, translate the sense of ourselves and others as that of faulty human beings to that of immortals in Christ. This is indeed the true meaning of atonement—that we, through the spiritualization of our thoughts, words, and deeds, shall become at one with Jesus Christ, *our true Selfhood*, and thus become one with God.

Desiring to give further light on this advanced and vitally important subject of individual man, we turn now to Jesus' parable of the Prodigal Son. We find that this particular parable, when spiritually interpreted, contains an intelligible explanation of the earthly life of the individual, and likewise its solution—that is, the price set for us each to pay in order that we may be awakened and reinstated in our right Mind and in our heavenly House (Consciousness) of peace, abundance, and happiness. So let us now take up this wonderful parable of the Master (Luke 15) and step by step interpret its spiritual meaning.

The younger son typifies you and me and every other soul on Earth, for do we not find ourselves in a world of materiality wherein everything originating in it is impermanent, destructible, and subject to annihilation? There is no doubt but that it is this man-made world which Jesus called "the far country," for here is where the son (man) "wasted his substance with riotous living." Indeed, our world today shows all too plainly the results of man's wasteful state of thinking and living, does it not?

The far country, this limited material existence, is not our true home nor our *rightful* place of living, and so, of necessity, both want and famine are experienced here; for if the son (man) should find lasting success and happiness in the things of the far country (this world), he would never long for, and ultimately return to, his true home—the consciousness of the kingdom of heaven at hand. So we find that because he met only with disappointment and distress, the son (man) now "joined himself to a citizen of that country." In like manner, we see man today, in his great desire and effort to find peace and plenty, continually looking to *others* for means of support and satisfaction.

The parable then continues: "And he would fain have filled his belly with the husks that the swine did eat." Have not many of us at times been so sorely tried and so desperately in need of peace and happiness that we have searched hither and yon for it—first in one thing and then another; applying to one person and then another—only to find in the end that "no man gave unto him," or us? And this is as it should be.

"And when he (man) came to himself, he said, How many hired servants of my father's have bread enough and to spare, and I perish here with hunger." The son then began to turn to the truth of the situation. He had reached the limit of his personal endurance, and in his dire extremity he contrasted his terrible condition of famine and want, of deprivation and despair, with the great plenty and the abundant good which rightfully belonged to him in his real home and true dwelling-place. We still hear his soul-awakened cry: "And I perish with hunger!"

It is thus with man today in this mortal experience of depression, lack, and limitation, asleep to his real place in Being. He too must "come to himself" by seeing that his suffering is *self-inflicted*! For why should any of us sit here bewailing our fate, looking to the world about us for food, funds, friends, life, health, happiness, only to find in the end that no man can really give them unto us? Why should we remain in such a low state of consciousness, deprived of so much that life holds dear and sweet, when all the while there is plenty for us all, and even to spare, in our true kingdom, *the Consciousness of God within us*?

All that the prodigal needed to do in order to contact his inexhaustible supply of the All-good was for him to "come to himself"—that is, open his consciousness and face the situation truly. Right here let us consider whether (as it would seem) our hunger today is for the meat and drink, the gold and silver, which this world can bestow upon us, or if our souls, like that of the prodigal, are crying out for their real food, the bread of Life, and for that true wealth of Life and Being which can be found only where it is really located—*in the Christ-nature of man*, who is actually your Being and mine whenever we embody Him.

Then what is the next step to take in consciousness after one makes this momentous and all-important discovery that the cause of his failure originates in *himself*? We find that Jesus, in his own inimitable way, gave us the peerless and all-inspiring answer in his simple words: "I will arise and go to my father, and will say unto him, Father, I have sinned against heaven and before you."

Yes indeed, when one really sees that his mistake is in ever trying to locate his wealth, his health, or his happiness *outside* himself in persons, places, and things external to him, and when he finally understands that this is actually the reason for all his "want" and his "famine," the deprivation of those things which he feels intuitively must rightfully belong to him, then he is willing to confess his folly to his Father within and also to the world without; for until one *acknowledges* his mistake, he is not in a position to make amends for it, nor to extricate himself from its painful conditions.

Then swiftly follows the next realization: "(I) am no more worthy to be called thy son: make me as one of thy hired servants." The heart has now been softened by suffering and purified by confession, and in his meekness and humility, the son has now reached the required state of individual spiritual receptivity.

Always, when one is sufficiently receptive to the truth which he should know and use at any particular time, he is able to hear it, and moreover, to feel it. "I will arise and go to my Father," cries out the son from his penitent and yearning heart and in the full and loving abandonment of the false self.

Contrariwise, many today expect the Father to first come unto them! They believe that the truth should snatch them right up out of the distressing circumstances and conditions in which they find themselves and set them down in a place of security where all good abounds, not knowing that such conditions were brought upon themselves by their own waywardness and ignorance, and can only be dissolved by their conforming with the true principle of life. In fact, it often happens that someone is greatly chagrined and even rebellious when he does not see this deliverance coming to pass in his life immediately.

Then again, man, in his ignorance of God's spiritual requirements of us all, often places the blame of his own shortcomings upon "the world, the flesh, and the devil." But Jesus in this parable so plainly tells us that it is the *individual man himself* who is responsible and who must turn his back on the past and face toward his Father's house—the one and only Source from which he will ever receive his rightful inheritance of eternal good.

Dear reader, can you see that each of us really has his true and perfect Being in the one infinite Jesus Christ, the all-inclusive and "only begotten Son," and that if we have wandered from this estate as in a dream, we must find our way back to it through an *awakening* or conversion which must take place in our consciousness? Can you see too that all that was needed in order for the son to be reinstated in his own true home, where an abundant supply of all good had ever awaited him, was for him to admit to himself his selfish mistake, then turn his humbled heart, his repentant feet, and his expectant face homeward—toward Reality?

You will note that the father came to meet the son, but not until the son had been willing to pay the price of Glory required of each and every individual soul.

So let us now, one and all, pause in introspection, and in the silence of our own hearts answer this crucial question: am I ready and willing to take the steps, whether they be few or many, which will lead me straight back to my Father's house, my true Consciousness of changeless perfection, where all the wonders and glories of the heavenly kingdom are prepared for me and for all since the foundation of the world? Am I ready and willing to follow the great principles of life—purity, love, honesty, and unselfishness—and so be ushered into a living experience of joy, peace, harmony, and the abundance of all good right here and now?

Our own true Being is our "father," or "king." Our "two sons" are our *mind* and our *heart*, which must ultimately be reconciled to each other and become obedient to us, their king. When we discern that there is but one Father of us all and one Lord of creation, then we shall also see that only as we lay down our life as a *personal* character in the Book of Life can we really be and act as the Lord-Self, the "author and finisher" of our own creations.

Chapter VIII

Awake and Choose Ye

The individual is always free to *accept* and *use* the insight and power of his true and genuine Being—the spiritual Man of God—or remain as he finds himself in the position of his limited human entity.

While everyone upon entering this world is essentially divine, he is born with a personal form subject to sin, sickness, and death; but at some point in his earthly experience, he may learn that he can transcend this form by way of the reality of himself as the Son of God. Then, if he chooses, he is in a position to rise out of the Adam-dream state into his real and true Christ estate. This balance of choice is what has been called the state of free will.

What, then, is the great need of the hour? "Now it is high time to awake out of sleep: for now is our salvation nearer than when we believed" (Rom. 13:11). We seem to need affliction and suffering as the most powerful means of arousing us from our long sleep in ignorance, until we learn how to *live* a life of goodness, honesty, purity, and love right on this Earth today.

Instead of praying for our suffering to cease, we should pray for the revelation of that which is causing the discordant condition to be expressed in our life. We can rest assured that God is always seeking us, and if we are not found of Him, then the reason for this must be with us. Most often the problem which we consider physical, social, or financial has to do altogether with an *adjustment* which must take place in our consciousness. Therefore, the *re-direction* of our thoughts and vision and the consequent *correction* of our conduct will break down that "middle wall of partition" which we have erected between ourselves and our good.

Many, deafened by the sins of the personal self, fail to hear the knocking of the meek and gentle Christ at the door of their hearts, and so they must learn only by the things which they suffer. But why should we who have had the benefit of this revelation accept discord of any kind or the limitation of any good thing, when our divine Self can so easily fulfill all our needs if we but live our daily lives in *harmony* with Him?

Our difficulties are really not stumbling blocks as they appear, but may be made the stepping-stones upon which we climb to a clearer atmosphere, a wider view, and a more perfect understanding of God's requirements of us. Our trials are like signals indicating our need of a more perfect unifying of our outer daily living with our inner spiritual ideals, and this is the price we all must pay—the willing crucifixion of the false, personal self with all its personal fears, doubts, ignorance, and sin; for remember, this personal self is the beginning and the end of all our troubles.

In the lives of many of us there comes a time when our inner and outer experiences cease to express that increased wealth of good which blessed our entrance into this new faith. *This is the time to give more attention to the study of the laws of spiritual unfoldment.* We cannot remain stationary in the new life but must be ever alert to regenerating ideas and their corresponding *forward moving impulses*. We are certain to hear the great invitation, "Come, ye blessed of my Father, inherit the kingdom prepared for you since the foundation of the world," if we have prepared ourselves for its high responsibilities and privileges.

Our human experiences may be bitter sometimes, and our lessons here severe; yet "in the twinkling of an eye," as the apostle says—in that instant when we resolve in ourselves to *live* the ideal life every instant of the day and to *be* that spiritual Man whom we have so long been reading and talking about—the tide of our earthly affairs will change for the better, and the longed-for experience of joy and happiness will be at hand. It may be in that very hour when you are turning from your problem, and with a single purpose beholding the true way set before you, that the light of His presence may directly shine upon you, revealing to you just where your thought or conduct needs correction and what is the next forward step which you should take.

As we call upon the Lord-Self to deliver us from our enemy, the personal man, and as we let the control of our earthly affairs rest upon His shoulders, behold! He changes the frightening and difficult places into glorious and new revelations and radiantly wonderful experiences for us. "Let not your heart be troubled: ye believe in God (the Father), believe also in me (your ever-present, perfect Selfhood)" (John 13:14). "No man cometh unto the Father, but by me" (John 14:16).

Then when shall we see the valley blossom as the rose for us? When shall we see the crooked places made straight for us? When shall we be able to "put off the old man with his deeds" and "put ye on the Lord Jesus Christ?" When we *stop* being the personal man of sin, doubt, fear, selfishness, sensitiveness, self-righteousness, and all the etceteras of the separated self, and *embody* and *manifest* the Man made in God's likeness, the Man who expresses the divine love of God!

None other than the living Christ in you can make all things "new" in your present experience. But how can He do this until you steadfastly recognize, love, and serve *Him* in yourself and in all others and cease to fear and to serve the false personal man?

Have not all of us had the experience of thinking, saying, and doing things that offended others and reacted harmfully upon our own state of mind and body, yet which, for a time, were unknown to us? How true it is then that men, the personal state, "knoweth not what they do." And is this not just what Jesus meant when he said, "He (the spirit of mischief in the personal man) was a murderer from the beginning." And again when referring, in metaphor, to man in his dream state, he said:

> Render to Caesar (the personal man) the things that are Caesar's (the thoughts and deeds which are in the category of person), and (render) to God the things that are God's (Matt. 22:21).

Dear seeker of Light, if in your past you have transgressed against another, then now is not too soon for you to confess your fault to him and ask forgiveness, for such action would be the loving fulfillment of that divine reconciliation. "If we confess our sins, he is faithful and just to forgive us our sins … (but) if we say that we have not sinned, we make him (Jesus) a liar, and his word is not in us" (1 John 1:9-10).

He who lives in the consciousness of his oneness with the Christ Selfhood is not troubled by "feelings" which are easily hurt; he does not take offense quickly, or indeed at all, for he knows that the Christ of himself, whom he is professing to follow and embody, has His vision ever turned to Reality and to the things of peace, love, harmony.

One might ask here, "If the Christ-Reality abides here and now in every soul, why is it that in spite of this, one may experience sin, sickness, and even death? Surely He could have no part in such conditions." You are right. This Self is within each individual—the all-victorious and ever-triumphant God-Being; supreme, divine, complete—and participates in no mortal or discordant condition whatsoever. But each of us must individually become at one with this true Self in our thoughts, in our affections, and in our daily living, if we would free ourselves from the evils of the personal man and experience the heavenly kingdom.

How can our sins be pardoned until they are corrected? And how can they be corrected until we are willing to confess them and let them go? Now, there is a way to live which insures success in every direction of life. It is to surrender the erring habits of thoughts and actions for the active expression of absolute love, absolute unselfishness, absolute purity, and absolute honesty in our every thought and deed—*the actual and conscious putting off of the human personality for the "altogether lovely" Jesus Christ.*

If we would be altogether free from sickness, then we must part with sin. If we would find happiness and prosperity, then we must be willing to live the kind and quality of a life which insures happiness and prosperity. Nor need we try to remove the "mote" from another's eye until we have first taken out the "beam" from our own. Our chief endeavor should not be to heal the sins of others, to enhance their happiness or bring about a larger degree of prosperity for them. Our chief endeavor and the greatest ambition in our whole life should be to live our own life to such a degree of *righteousness*—harmony, love, virtue, and goodness—that we will be a living witness to our Father and a true inspiration to others to bring them to the same source of Glory.

> Let your light so shine before men, that they may see your good works, and glorify your Father which is in heaven (Matt. 5:16).
> I, if I be lifted up from the earth, will draw all men unto me (John 12:32).

Dear friends, there is no real, true, or permanent way to obtain the freedom of a life of health, happiness, and prosperity here on Earth other than by embodying in your own individual disposition and conduct, your own heart and soul and being, the very nature and identity of Jesus Christ. Plainly did he tell us that many other ways and means would be presented to us, ways which would seem so like unto his own sublimely perfect way that even the "elect" of us might be deceived. But he stated boldly and authoritatively that He Himself was, and is, the *only* perfect way; that His way of becoming "reborn" and molded anew into His life, His spirit, His disposition, His nature, His character, His conduct, verily His own Being, is the only one *perfect* way to the kingdom.

> Except ye be converted, and become as little children, ye shall not enter into the kingdom of heaven. ... I am the door: by me if any man enter in, he shall be saved. ... As the branch cannot bear fruit of itself, except it abides in the vine; no more can ye, except ye abide in me. ... Seek ye first the kingdom of God, and his righteousness, and all these things shall be added unto you.

Let us see now what meaning the dictionary gives of this word *righteousness*: "the quality of being good; virtuous; innocent; conforming in disposition and conduct to the divine standard of right." Now then, as we seek first of all to conform our disposition and conduct to absolute goodness, peace, justice, mercy, honesty, purity, and unselfishness, we are thereby entering into the kingdom of heaven, and as the "things" of happiness, health, harmony, and abundance of all good are right there, already prepared for us, they are naturally "added" unto us. Is this not an illuminating and transcending vision, tearing aside the veils of personality which would keep us from consciously *living, acting,* and *being* that very Jesus-nature which we have been professing to love and worship?

So, dear one, stop trying to be healed of this or that disease of body or disease of limitation, but instead be born of the Spirit. Be the kingdom of heaven in your disposition, in your conduct, and in your every association with mankind. The kingdom of peace, harmony, joy, and abundance is neither "lo here or, lo there!" for behold, it is to be found, to be loved, and to be lived *right in your very own Self and Being.* The sooner you find it and the sooner you embody it the sooner also will you have the lovely things of heaven and of Earth added to you. If this wonderful life of Glory is worth anything to us, is it not worth our all?

Think of the homes which have been disrupted and the families which have been separated because certain members began to preach to others their idea of the kingdom of heaven before they had embodied this kingdom in their own lives. Nor need we leave our homes or our dear ones in order to be shining lights to others. On the contrary, "Charity begins at home." Listen to our Master's authority on this point:

> Thou hypocrite, first cast out the beam out of thine own eye; and then shalt thou see clearly to cast out the mote out of thy brother's eye (Matt. 7:5).

As one gives up his life to Spirit, he must necessarily begin to practice the new life right in his own home, right where he finds himself, no matter where that place is. No need to try to convert others by any means other than by oneself—one's own evangelized and *spiritualized* disposition, nature, and conduct. When we have purified our own consciousness of vain imaginations, egotism, and the multitudinous forms of mortal selfishness, and are endeavoring to express the basic principles of life, such as perfect love, purity, and unselfishness, then indeed are we "shining lights" which will draw others into the same consciousness. In what better way can we help the world? Verily, the standard of Jesus Christ, individually embodied and expressed, will be the very means of bringing the millennium on Earth today.

How many of you who read this book are seeking to demonstrate over the pain and disease, over the unhappiness and misery, over the lack and limitation in your own lives today? Then hear ye! The day of making demonstrations over evil conditions is now coming to a close. The day of seeking for the "added things" is now drawing to its end. Moreover, the day of *teaching* the word of Life after this fashion must now give place to that divine standard of *right living* which transcends teaching of every kind.

Listen closer: such is not the real approach to that kingdom which is within us, and this is the reason why your sickness or affliction has not vanished and why your lack or limitation has not been replaced with the abundance of every good thing.

Turn yourself to the Master's own teaching! What does He say? "Seek ye first the kingdom of God, and his righteousness; and all these things shall be added unto you." Is it any wonder, then, that you have not received your good? Until you stop praying for your body to be healed, your home to be blessed, and your purse to be filled, you have not yet learned the real truth of your Being.

Seek ye first the kingdom of righteousness in yourself! Begin first of all to attune your disposition and conduct to the gentle, tender, compassionate, ever-forgiving and all-loving Jesus Christ! Let your light—your *actions* and your *deeds*—shine forth with the brightness of *His* glory; then you will have no need to "demonstrate" the supply of any good thing, for lo, you will find it already added unto you and manifested now right where you stand.

Awake, sleeping souls, and turn yourselves to the Light. Seek not only to read the Bible, which presents the truth of life to you, but seek to *be* the Bible and to *be* the truth of life right in your very own experience! Seek not only to learn about the "altogether lovely" Jesus Christ, but seek to *be* the altogether lovely Jesus Christ, right where you stand! Seek not only to have the joys and blessings of the regenerated life, but seek to *be* that regenerated life *here and now*!

Is not this the glorious message of Jesus to the prodigal world today? "Come unto me, all ye that labor and are heavy laden, and I will give you rest. ... My yoke is easy, and my burden is light." Yes, the true Way, *lived and practiced*, will bring us all gently, easily, swiftly into the experience of heaven on Earth.

Ever calls the tenderly persuasive voice: "Follow me, and I will make you fishers of men." Instead of spending our time in trying to get health, prosperity, or any other good thing, we should know that all such blessings will be added unto us naturally if we but follow Jesus' teachings; and besides this, we will be able to become "fishers of men"; that is, others will see our good works, and they too will begin to glorify "our Father which art in heaven."

Therefore, awake and "choose you this day whom ye will serve" (Josh. 24:15). "How long halt ye between two opinions? if the Lord be God, follow him: but if Baal, then follow him" (1 Kings 18:20).

> Not every one that saith unto me, Lord, Lord, shall enter into the kingdom of heaven; but he that doeth the will of my Father which is in heaven.
>
> Many will say to me in that day, Lord, Lord, have we not prophesied in thy name? and in thy name have cast out devils? and in thy name done many wonderful works?
>
> And then will I profess unto them, I never knew you: depart from me, ye that work iniquity.
>
> Therefore whosoever heareth these sayings of mine, and doeth them, I will liken him unto a wise man, which built his house upon a rock:
>
> And the rain descended, and the floods came, and the winds blew, and beat upon that house; and it fell not: for it was founded upon a rock.
>
> And every one that heareth these sayings of mine, and doeth them not, shall be likened unto a foolish man, which built his house upon the sand:
>
> And the rain descended, and the floods came, and the winds blew, and beat upon that house; and it fell: and great was the fall of it (Matt. 7:21-27).

Truly a phenomenal change takes place in that one who constantly strives to live and act in at-one-ment with the Jesus Christ Consciousness. His whole nature radiates divine love, sweet reasonableness, and true helpfulness. Critical or harsh words are never spoken by him and, if spoken heretofore, are repented of and wiped from his memory; arguments and bickerings cease. He now sees that he must forgive others if he himself would be forgiven of God. So "bury the dead (past)" and reach up and on to the glorious, free life of the Spirit—the ever-triumphant and all-victorious Jesus experience.

In the "far country," which is the man-made world, we all share in the common dream of separation from our real Consciousness (our Father) and our true Selfhood (Jesus Christ); but it is not a true or eternal separation, inasmuch as all of us shall inevitably return to our perfect estate. Man cannot, however, of his personal or human self, ever find the way back to the kingdom but must be drawn by the Father, for Jesus said, "No man cometh unto me (the Christ of himself) unless the Father draw him."

When one feels that yearning desire for peace and harmony or the inner urge for freedom, when he feels drawn to the beauty of nature about him and to the things and thoughts of the life of Spirit, he may then know that God is calling him to leave the far country of the *personal self* and make his way back to his real home and Being.

Often the question is asked why it is that conditions seem more difficult after one has received the call of Spirit than before. The reason may be because he has not responded fully enough or surrendered enough. He may still be clinging unconsciously to the thoughts and ways of his own personality. When he releases himself more definitely and thoroughly from materiality and personality by identifying himself persistently with his own indwelling Christ-Being, he will then be in a position to claim his inheritance as the Son of God and thus create his own good "in earth as in heaven."

Verily, verily, each moment requires of us to *choose* where we shall place our vision; whether we shall deal with the Jesus-nature of ourselves and of others or the Caesar appearance; whether we shall "purge out therefore the old leaven, that ye may be a new lump, as ye are unleavened" or be longer kept from becoming conscious partakers of the "inheritance incorruptible."

> Hereby know we the spirit of truth, and the spirit of error ... No (personal) man hath seen God at any time. If we love one another, God dwelleth in us, and his love is perfected in us ... God accepteth no man's person ... for (in reality) ye are all one in Christ Jesus (1 John 4:6; 4:12; Gal. 2:6; 3:28).

"Satan" is the spirit of personality which "goeth to and fro in the earth" and "as a roaring lion, walketh about, seeking whom he may devour" (Job 1:7; 1 Pet. 5:8). But rest assured, dear ones, his beginning and end is oblivion. He cannot prevail against the Jesus-nature of man, for it is written:

> And the great dragon was cast out, that old serpent, called the Devil, and Satan, which deceiveth the whole world; he was cast out into the earth (oblivion), and his angels (thoughts and deeds of personality) were cast out with him.
> And I heard a loud voice saying in heaven, Now is come salvation, and strength, and the kingdom of our God, and the power of his Christ: for the accuser of our brethren is cast down, which accused them before our God day and night.
> And I saw a new heaven and a new earth: for the first heaven (in the sky) and the first earth (human consciousness) were passed away; and there was no more sea (trouble).
> And there shall be no more curse: but the throne of God and of the Lamb shall be in it; and his servants shall serve him:
> And they shall see his face; and his name (Jesus Christ) shall be in their foreheads (Rev. 12:9-10; 21:1; 22:3-4).

Chapter IX

Ourselves and Others

In both the Old and New Testament, we are told that the first and greatest of all the commandments is this: "Thou shalt love the Lord thy God with all thy heart, and with all thy soul, and with all thy mind" (Matt. 32:27). Since the Christ within us is our only approach to our perfect and our complete good, it is evident that we must first of all love and serve this Christ in *ourselves*; then we shall be in a position to love and serve this same Christ in others. "For ye are all one in Christ Jesus" (Gal. 3:28) ... "members one of another" (Eph. 4:25).

Since he, the indivisible inner Man, is already the supreme of each of us, we have only to *turn* from the human, or personal self of us, and *surrender* to this ever-present and ever waiting Christ-Reality of us to receive the blessing. What could sooner bring wars to an end; what better bring the sins and sorrows of all nations to their oblivious conclusion than the *re-adjustment* of man himself who made them? This he can do only as he obeys the command: be freed from self—be Me!

The time for us all to be ready to pay the price of Glory in order to live the perfect life of truth and love is right upon us! Loving and understanding the one Being of us all will help us to express our divine characteristics in true service. Read again in John's Gospel (chapter thirteen) the story of that hour when our divine Master "girded himself with a towel" and, in an unparalleled manner of gracious service, displayed his divine love for humanity, saying impressively unto his disciples, "I have given you an example that ye should do as I have done to you." Only as man is actuated by the characteristics of Jesus Christ can he dissolve in love the discords of Earth. In relinquishing all else for this, his true Being, he has chosen "that good part, which shall not be taken away" (Luke 10:42).

So see yourself, dear one, now and right where you are, as taking leave of the dream experience of separateness because you are now waking to the real truth of your inseparable oneness with God, your Author and Being. Hold steadfastly to this vision in your everyday thinking, living, and acting, and in good time you will find the disturbing dream experience of lack or limitation giving place to the certainty of your divine and ever-harmonious Selfhood; for surely there is a way, for those who leave all for it, leading to "the secret place of the most High" wherein they shall ever "abide under the shadow of the Almighty."

What is not right in our earthly experience, the miracle-working Christ which we "put on" can make right for us. He can make the crooked straight, the sick well, the sinful pure, the poor rich, and the weak strong. Yea, releasing ourselves from the mortal man state, or the material dream existence, through willing self-surrender, we shall each, here and now, progress not only into the true understanding of our Life and Being but likewise toward the full experience of it.

For our God is health and harmony and cannot know discord; God is all Good and cannot know evil. To know that He abides in the midst of every individual soul today, awaiting only our whole allegiance to Him in the intensely yearning desire to manifest Him, is to set us free from our bondage to every ill. "And ye shall seek me, and find me, when ye shall search for me with all your heart" (Jer. 29:13).

Many seem confused about the right mental attitude to hold in relation to the faults or sins of others, as well as to the persons themselves. We should first of all learn to separate sin from the sinner. To hate the sin but feel absolute love for the sinner is the correct attitude of awareness.

> Ye that love the Lord, hate evil (Ps. 97:10). Hate evil, love good (Amos: 5:15).

Who is the sinner? you ask. You know, of course, that he is not the indwelling Christ, the manifested mind of God. You have been shown too that he is not the mortal man, for he is the effect and not the cause of sin. The sinner is none other than the individual soul acting unwisely in his unawakened and unredeemed state of consciousness.

Jesus came on Earth to destroy sin but to save the sinner! As the sinner is twice-born, he will separate himself from sin and become a "new creature" right here on Earth. "I came not to call the righteous, but sinners to repentance," instructed the Master; thus, it was written of him, "Behold ... a friend of ... sinners!" (Luke 7:34). As we learn how to keep the sin and the sinner separated in our consciousness, we too shall be able to save sinners and instruct them into the way of righteousness.

> He which converteth the sinner from the error of his way shall save a soul from death, and shall hide a multitude of sins (Jas. 5:20).
> Likewise, I say unto you, there is joy in the presence of the angels of God over one sinner that repenteth (Luke 15:10).

Surely one of the hardest lessons we have to learn is to see our loved ones following in the wrong paths of unwisdom, by acting in opposition to the true standards of life, and to hold our loving patience, knowing that God will ultimately become known to them; for we know that it is not our privilege to snatch them as "a brand plucked out of the fire" and so protect them from the natural results of their erring ways. We cannot direct their feet in the path of righteousness unless they themselves are willing to *renounce* that way of blind ignorance or willful sin which they have been following.

It is important that we lose not our own poise or our serenity by reacting antagonistically or sorrowfully to another's ignorant or willful waywardness. This may be a most difficult lesson for us to learn—not to act in disappointment, in resentment, or in unforgiveness to those who do not appear to be living in harmony with the Christ standard; but this practice of right perception, when learned, will prove to be the inner help and stimulus which our loved one needs in his progress toward a better understanding of life, and at the same time it will greatly advance us spiritually.

How else could we expect to reach our own perfection except by the spiritualization, transfiguration, and ascension of our individual consciousness? And how can this take place in us except as we repent of, renounce, and surrender all in ourselves which is opposed to the mind which is in Christ Jesus—our God-Being?

You yourself must decide whether you are going to continue to suffer because of another's wrong thoughts and actions, or whether you now understand how to separate sin from the sinner. We have all placed ourselves, more or less, in a system of circumstances which keeps revolving in an orbit of disappointment, suffering, and sorrow about the personal self until we are ready to part company with that self who is but the mortal and the unreal of us and who, because of the offending conduct of others, would feel hurt, resentful, or unforgiving. But here is our great opportunity to extricate ourselves from this kind of suffering, by refusing to be any longer that deluded mortal who entertains such feelings! Verily, this is the cross by which we gain the crown. Therefore, "Hold that fast which thou hast (the new perception), that no man take thy crown (thy peace and blessedness)" (Rev. 3:11).

As long as we are disturbed by the conduct of other persons, so long are we too living in a state of ignorance and subject to its penalties. If we resent or resist the selfishness of another, we need to search more deeply within ourselves for that holy place of peace where the pure Christ alone reigns and where we may definitely prove that "Greater is he that is in you, than he that is in the world" (1 John 4:4).

It is not the kindest course, as it would seem, to try to improve or to spiritualize the man who is not yet convinced that his search for freedom and happiness in the "far country" must ever prove unsuccessful and tragically fruitless. Better always, though painful sometimes, to let him discover for himself that nothing but famine and want await those who choose the barren ways of the separate self to the completeness and perfection of that Being who is the Author of us all.

As we progress on the straight and narrow pathway, rich faith, divine patience, and sublime courage must be our constant companions, for there is much to be removed and much to be added in consciousness before the divine likeness is experienced and made manifest in us. By detaching ourselves from the personal man of us, we continually rise into the higher consciousness of our inner Christ-Reality and so into loftier aims and happier experiences.

Our abandonment of the personal self is our only release from sin and suffering of all kinds, for the expression of a personality separate from the One enfolds all the conditions of sin, sickness, and death with which we are acquainted. Christ-purified, His peace and harmony shall be ours; Christ-governed, His power and wisdom shall be added unto us, and all that we do shall prosper.

No real progress in mind and heart can ever be made without the sacrifice of the unlovely thoughts and things of the personal self; and every time this self is laid on the altar, we are that much nearer the end of that mental separation existing between ourselves and our experience of perfection. Ever asks the Christ, "Wilt thou lay down thy life for my sake?"

Dear seeker, can you detach yourself enough from personality to search yourself diligently and impartially and make a mental list of the selfish qualities in your disposition? Then, like the experienced gardener who fertilizes his soil to put it in a good state of cultivation, can you improve your disposition by permeating your consciousness with the spiritual qualities of loving-kindness, tenderness, patience, unselfishness, and compassion? Moreover, you must eradicate from your thoughts and conversation the choking brambles of gossip, criticism, and condemnation which pertain to the human personality.

Remember to keep uppermost in consciousness that, in order to deal most understandingly with others, we must deal first with ourselves, and the paramount concern of the moment to us all should be: what progress am I making in putting off that self which is my person and functioning in that Self which is my *Christ-Reality*? For we know that "God accepteth no man's person" (Gal. 2:6). Practice faithfully the resolution of St. Paul, who said, "For I am determined not to know (accept) anything among you, save Jesus Christ." The more progress we can make in this exercise the sooner can we fulfill the complete requirement and receive Him, "the hope of glory," and thus be reinstated in our real home and Being.

Our unchanging and only Good stands always ready and waiting for us, but we must first take those steps which lead us back to the Father's house. The good which the prodigal sought was the very identical good which he had left, for such things as permanent happiness, harmony, health, and holiness are of Spirit, spiritual, and not of person, personal.

There are many people who retard their spiritual progress by not seeing the great importance of *turning from all else to depend on God*. They say, "I try so hard, but I cannot seem to realize the truth." Search more diligently, dear one, and look more intently into yourself to see what it is that is standing between yourself and God. To remain in the mental realm of mere thoughts and statements of good, while all the time your soul is crying out for its pure satisfaction in the Christ Himself, keeps you in a confused and discontented state of consciousness, for the soul is longing for the *all* of Spirit, while the mind is working in its limited dimensions. The soul can never be satisfied with anything less than the all of Spirit, for "it is the spirit that quickeneth; the flesh profiteth nothing" (John 6:63). Again we read, "For what shall it profit a man, if he shall gain the whole world, and lose his own soul? Or what shall a man give in exchange for his soul?" (Mark 8:36-37).

Only in proportion as one turns from the modern forms of iniquity and idolatry to find joy in his spiritual perfection in "the firstborn of every creature," will he gradually lose his adherence to the dream-life of mortality, with all its painful and distressing pictures, and experience that fulness and completeness for which he is seeking.

Much discord and confusion spring up today in the minds of those who see the truth intellectually but not by way of the heart and who seek the gifts of the spiritual life without being willing to surrender every vestige of self in order to gain them. "Beware lest any man spoil you through philosophy and vain deceit, after the tradition of men, after the rudiments of the world, and not after Christ" (Col. 2:8).

We need not be limited to instruction from books and teachers. When one's heart is sufficiently receptive to receive the things of Spirit, he may be instructed directly from the "inner Christ-Man." The revelation of Truth is not confined to persons or times. The intuitive man admits that infinite, ever-present God is the source of all knowledge, and so he should also see that the receiver of this knowledge is as free as the Giver is free.

How can man ever set his world to rights until he has first adjusted the world within himself? And how can he adjust this in any way other than by unifying his thoughts, emotions, and actions continually with those of the inner Christ-Man? To claim your rights as the spiritual Man and then not live in close accord with Him brings discord and confusion into your life; for if you would claim your right to health, wealth, or happiness and harmony, *you must be that Man who has such rights and privileges*! In order, for instance, to enjoy the rights and privileges of a citizen of the United States, one must first of all be that citizen, must he not?

The spiritual Man has no personal mind or will of his own, for his mind is the mind of God, and his will is the will of God; in fact, the spiritual Man is one with God in all things and in all ways. For it is written:

> The Son can do nothing of himself, but what he seeth the Father do: for what things soever he doeth, these also doeth the Son likewise ... For as the Father hath life in himself, so hath he given to the Son to have life in himself (John 5:19, 26).

Man, consciously expressing the intelligence of God, does not choose between good and evil, right and wrong—he knows the good and the right only. Nor is there any evil known to the Christ-Man, for "unto the pure all things are pure" (Tit. 1:15). He can enjoy the beautiful things of Life always, for he knoweth, "For thy pleasure they are and were created" (Rev. 4:11). Indeed, the spiritual Son is free as God is free; He is perfect as God is perfect; for Father and Son, Author and his Character, are the same one. "He that seeth me seeth him that sent me" (John 12:45).

It may be asked, "If we are really this spiritual Man, God's image and likeness, then why can we not be freed from sickness, from sin, and from all forms of limitation here and now?" We can, if we will but embody Him. It is not enough to mentally claim our birthright and assert our real Sonship, but we must likewise live, act, and be the perfect Man in our thoughts and in our conduct.

The spiritual Man cannot be sick, cannot sin, and cannot be afraid. He is the very incarnation of God. He is the Word made flesh, and he has no will or power to think or to feel separate or apart from God. Therefore, with all our hearts, let us *believe, receive, and embody our Christ-Self* as our perfect, changeless Life, as the unalterable Truth, and as boundless, unchanging Love. So shall we enjoy one Mind, one Life, and one Experience.

There are those who find themselves in a state of mental confusion at times, believing that the cause for such condition lies in circumstances quite outside their control. However, the worry or the troubled mind which one feels should be like a danger signal to him, indicating that he is on the wrong track; that he should stop and carefully consider the direction which his thoughts are taking regarding the matter before him. When we place our faith and confidence in the power of persons and things, we are living out of harmony with our true inner estate, and so naturally there must arise in us a reaction, or a disturbed mental state, and this signal has been called *worry*.

It is generally conceded that it is wrong to worry, but as one rightly understands its origin and nature, he will be able to eliminate it by absorbing its lesson. Troubled thoughts should be an indication that one is thinking or doing something in the wrong way; for if he will search his own consciousness, he will discover that he is misplacing the power which rightfully belongs to the Christ character in persons and things, and naturally they now assume control over him.

One loses his sense of Self-control when he places the Christ-power, which he naturally possesses over his health, in any person, place, or thing. This is also true regarding his happiness, for in his inherent right he has the power in himself, through his at-one-ment with the Christ, to preserve his own happiness. But if he gives over this power to others, then in his ignorance he believes they are causing him to be unhappy and dejected. With prosperity or success too, the power to be rich lies in one's own Being, But if he is ignorant of this and instead places this power in persons, places, and things outside the Christ—in himself—then he temporarily loses control over his wealth, and not knowing the reason, he worries and is troubled about his affairs.

When a man looks to this world for his health, his wealth, or his happiness, that is, when he places his health in the physical body, his wealth in material possessions, and his happiness in human personalities, he is ignorant of the fact that these spiritual realities—health, wealth, and happiness—are not products of the personal man nor of the material world but are creations of the true Man, the one Jesus Christ whom we should all embody. Paul discerned this when he wrote, "God created all things by Jesus Christ" (Eph. 3:9).

Because of false education, most people look upon money, for instance, as a material substance, something outside themselves; whereas, the true idea of wealth is that it is a concept of the divine Man within us. As a human being, one creates material things, but as a spiritual Being he may create spiritual things. That is, we may create our own good right where we now stand if we will but fulfill the necessary divine requirements.

When man gives up his personality and embodies in thought, word, and action his real Being as the only begotten of the Father, then he is in the position of at-onement with Christ—one in power, one in dominion and glory, and as Jesus illustrated, one also in the ability to multiply and create every specific form of his needful supply.

Not understanding the spiritual nature of his material wealth (for all *good* things of Earth have their origin in Spirit) but believing it to be the result of his own personal success, man is subject to the fluctuating conditions of the material world and is hence at its mercy. But his material loss can be his spiritual gain if he will but realize and correct his mistaken concept of wealth and, turning from all his old beliefs about it, begin to practice the inherent, creative power bestowed upon him "from the foundation of the world."

Often when man reaches an extremity, when he finds that nothing either physical or mental can save him from poverty, sickness, or despair, he instinctively turns completely away from man and his powerless attempts of deliverance; then the Father, by way of his own Christ within, is given the opportunity to save him. Many of us have found that in a state of great desperation, when we have been driven into a place where there seems no hope on any side, when we have utterly abandoned the idea of help from any earthly source, then quite suddenly and unexpectedly a Light dawned in our consciousness; our darkness has been illumined, and swifter than any earthly deliverance could be, the trouble vanished.

The risen Jesus employed no means of the material world to heal his lacerated hands or his pierced side, nor to weave new raiment for him; the Christ in himself was his all-sufficient Creator. And this Christ-light within ourselves will create for us such things as we need today, if we will but awaken from our long sleep and learn to use the creative powers of our own Being.

Only as we are able to detach ourselves from the mortal personality of us and from our mortal thinking, shall we be able to transpose ourselves from the many forms of bondage and limitation into the true expression of plenty, peace, harmony, and happiness. Only as we waken out of the long sleep to transcend our ignorance of Life eternal shall we be enabled to raise ourselves from mortality to immortality; from corruption to incorruption; from imperfect human beings to the spiritual Christ-Man—the individual in his true position.

Indeed, we shall then stand awake in the likeness and very Being of the kingly Self, the Author of our existence. Our experience as a character asking for "the portion of goods that falleth to me" and eating "of the tree of the knowledge of (both) good and evil" will be ended.

Chapter X

Healing in His Name

What man save our Lord Jesus Christ ever trod this Earth saying that we could be healed of all our false views of life and of all our sins and troubles *in his name*? He gave us his own name as our *deliverance* from ills of every kind, even from death itself. He said:

> I am the resurrection, and the life: he that believeth in me, though he were dead, yet shall he live: and whosoever believeth in me shall never die. Believest thou this?

Jesus knew that the reason why we can be redeemed in his name only is that his name is the real name of every individual soul, the common Identity of us all. Just as in one's signature lies concealed his personal identity, Jesus taught that only as one knows his true name, *and lives in harmony and accord with it*, does he free himself from any evil whatsoever.

"As many as received him, to them gave he power to become (in full consciousness) the sons of God, even to them that believe on his name" (John 1:12). "Whatsoever ye shall ask in my name, that will I do, that the Father may be glorified in the Son" (John 14:13).

Let us rest no longer content with merely reading and talking about our at-one-ment with the Christ, but rather, let us now take the next step forward and be in our earthly experience what we have always been in our heavenly reality—this Son who is the Father in expression. We need no longer play the part of the pitiful prodigal, when our whole being yearns to return to that perfect estate which is our inseparable but long-forgotten oneness with the Father. *It rests with each of us to decide when he is ready to begin the work of rebirth and redemption and to advance into the perfection of the Son "in whom all fulness dwells."*

You may be asking yourself, "How can that Jesus who lived two thousand years ago heal me of my fears, my troubles, and my limitations today? How can his name take away my darkness and bring me light, take away my cares and tribulations and bring me into the kingdom of heaven here and now?

The name alone, or as a mere word, cannot do this for you, dear one, until you open up your *mind* and *heart* to its full and complete meaning and spiritually perceive that Jesus Christ is the name of the Man "made in the image and likeness of God"—the Character who is the Author, *our perfect Selfhood and our true Identity.* By living and acting *in disposition and conduct,* in consistency with this true Identity of us all, we shall gradually free ourselves from the mortal dream state of the personal life with its multitudinous limitations.

"If the Son therefore shall make you free, you shall be free indeed" (John 8:36). Jesus paid the supreme price of Glory in order to reveal to man his true Identity. "For ye are bought with a price," announced Paul. Jesus came into this world to waken us from sleep, to free us from bondage, and to show us that our way back to our original state of perfection can be consummated only by our coalescence with him—our true Being. "For this cause came I unto this hour" (John 12:27).

"No man knoweth the Son, but the Father; neither knoweth any man the Father, save the Son, and he to whomsoever the Son will reveal him" (Mark. 11:27). The Son is the *medium* through which invisible Spirit becomes *visible* form, Life becomes *intelligent* activity, and the I AM becomes *individualized* characterization.

To believe that we have life in God, but willing to leave our thought of it in the formless and the intangible, is not enough to furnish us with the continuous enjoyment of health and an uninterrupted abundance of joy and happiness in our lives today, any more than for us to understand that there is plenty of electricity in the power house would be sufficient to bring its light and heat into our homes! No, the electric energy must express itself in action and in power through forms made ready for it; then, and then only, can we make practical use of it.

> In like manner, if we expect the Spirit of Jesus Christ to appear in our lives today, we must surrender to him our hearts and our minds as the medium through which he may manifest as our visible health, our abundance, and our serene happiness—in fact, everything in our earthly experience should testify to our perfect surrender to the indivisible Christ and to the regenerative power of his Presence in us all.

The power of God, the love of God, the substance of God are all in our very own Savior (Jesus) Self, and it rests with us individually to consciously put on "the Lord Jesus Christ" *by manifesting and expressing in our disposition and conduct* his qualities of Being. "Whatsoever a man soweth, that shall he also reap" announces the mental law which operates in the lives of all of us until we make a full surrender of the personal man. If one's disposition and conduct are contrary to the great principles of true Manhood and right living, he is bound to reap the result called lack and limitation.

"Be not deceived; God is not mocked," for whatsoever quality a man soweth in his thought, his disposition, and his conduct, that same quality shall he experience in his bodily and external affairs, until he learns how to live in that true state of Consciousness wherein this law cannot operate. As he becomes "twice-born," born of the Spirit as well as of the flesh, he gradually conforms his thoughts and actions to the true standards of right living here on Earth. Then this Christ, *experienced in himself*, is the end of that mental law for him. Thus, true "healing" applies *primarily* to the inner heart and soul of man, and the *effects* of such—a right change of consciousness and conduct evidenced forth as health, wealth, and happiness—will follow naturally and inevitably.

It makes such a great difference how we express ourselves—whether we manifest, or express, that personal, temporary self of us or that immortal, changeless Christ of us; whether as weak mortals we strive to advance toward perfection, which all the while seems somehow to evade us, or if as the "twice-born" we are able to see with the beloved disciple that "the Son of God is come, and hath given us an understanding, that we may know him that is true, and we are in him that is true, even in his Son Jesus Christ. This is the true God, and eternal life" (1 John 5:20).

The state called heaven is not something to be sought outside and acquired by us as though it were not already existing within us essentially, awaiting *recognition* and *expression*. The King and His kingdom are one and inseparable and are both within us, and in proportion as we let go of the Adam-man, and his thoughts and actions, for the Christ-Man of our heavenly perfection, shall we surely experience the joys of the kingdom of God within us, our rightful inheritance.

"New wine must be put into new bottles," announced our Lord and Master. This perfect and regenerative idea of becoming "twice-born" men, the altogether "new creature," must be recognized and accepted as the prerequisite of that great spiritual awakening which is required on Earth today.

> Know ye not that the unrighteous shall not inherit the kingdom of God? Be not deceived: neither fornicators, nor idolaters, nor adulterers, nor effeminate, nor abusers of themselves with mankind, nor thieves, nor covetous, nor drunkards, nor revilers, nor extortioners, shall inherit the kingdom of God (1 Cor. 6:9-10).
>
> Put on the new man, which after God is created in righteousness and true holiness ... Put on the whole armor of God, that ye may be able to stand against the wiles of the devil. For we wrestle not against flesh and blood, but against principalities, against powers, against the rulers of the darkness of this world, against spiritual wickedness in high places (Eph. 4:24; 6:11-12).

Then why should we delay another hour to turn within and find this Self who is "closer than breathing, nearer than hands and feet" and His kingdom of heaven which is ever at hand? Why not begin now to experience in our daily lives, and show forth to the world at large, the true gospel—*the good news that this one king and this one kingdom are within reach of us all*?

Verily, the enlightened ministry which *recognizes and practices* the *one* Presence in the universe—of whom are all things, from whom are all things, and in whom are all things—will ultimately teach all men how to transcend the material and mental modes and methods of help whereby they seek to heal their own self-inflicted wounds, miseries, and limitations, and will reveal the true way to cancel all sin and its painful consequences and "put to flight the armies of the aliens," the host of evil beliefs and conditions, "for the word of God is quick, and powerful, and sharper than any two-edged sword" (Heb. 4:12).

> It is only the ministry that recognizes and preaches the putting on of the new life through rebirth and regeneration within us that can ever penetrate the thick

darkness of ignorance in many minds, due to misconception, and lo! man partakes again of his long-lost estate held in trust by his Father.

"Behold, I make all things new!" exclaims He of the great Revelation. When man ceases to look upon evil in his world as something substantial and inevitable, recognizing it as only the "invention" of the unawakened soul, hence temporal and self-imposed, it will begin to vanish into its nothingness as darkness does before the light. Sin, sickness, death, and all forms of bondage and limitation are not realities of God or manifestations of the inner Christ-Man, but are inventions of men who do not unify themselves in thought and action with the true standards of living, for "Lo, God hath made man upright; but they have sought out many inventions" (Eccles. 7:29).

"For as in Adam (*the self-imposed human state*) all die, even so in Christ (*the natural and perfect state*) shall all be made alive" (1 Cor. 15:22). As it is seen and accepted that the Christ-state was originally, and is, ever intrinsically ours, we begin to live and walk in a new world. *Believest thou this*? Then accept this God-created and God-crowned Man as supreme in yourself by living in accord with him: for it is only through our *individual embodiment of this indwelling Christ-Man* that we shall ever gain the permanent victory over sin, over sickness, over all forms of limitation and vicissitudes of the earth-consciousness of man.

How we should rejoice to be released from the penalties of "the laws of sin and death," that we may have access, by faith, unto grace!

We have already painfully learned the "letter" of that law, "line upon line, precept upon precept," as when in kindergarten we learned to compute by means of beads and blocks. But, similarly, as we advanced from this elementary method of counting into the higher grades of mathematics, so should we progress from our dependence upon various doctrines and beliefs into the *full and complete knowledge of the Spirit*, which is "Christ in you, the hope of glory."

It will be remembered that when we left the kindergarten and gave up counting by means of blocks and beads, having learned to compute without them, nevertheless we retained the knowledge gained therefrom. So in this more advanced grade of *spiritual understanding*, we find that the letter of "right thinking" will be absorbed into the higher understanding of *true living*. Then the brilliancy of the Christ-light will automatically draw our eyes away from "the wisdom of this world, which is foolishness with God." Graduated into this higher understanding of righteous living, we shall walk by the light of the Christ, who is "the end of the (mental) law."

No prejudiced criticism or condemnation should ever be thought or felt toward other religious teachings on Earth today, for they are all traveling toward the same goal—heaven. But nothing can ever bring all religions of the world together into the perfect whole except man's embodiment of the ageless, universal Christ, who is his savior and redeemer, truly the one and only begotten Son of God, "where there is neither Greek nor Jew, circumcision nor uncircumcision, Barbarian, Scythian, bond nor free: but Christ is all, and in all" (Col. 3:11).

Through spiritual realization and the conscious practice of righteousness in our everyday living, we see Good in everything and become like the crystal which reflects in light all the objects about it. Then, and not until then, do we "all come in the unity of the faith, (seeing all life as one) and of the knowledge of the Son of God, unto a perfect man, unto the measure of the stature of the fulness of Christ" (Eph. 4:13).

Man today, laboring physically and mentally to bring healing to himself and others, can never accomplish the wonders which can be brought forth by simple application of the great principles which represent the true standards of living, such as perfect love, unselfishness, sincerity, and virtue. The way that we, individually, work out our own salvation is none other than by *being the conscious embodiment of perfect Life, Truth, and Love.*

When one has surrendered the personal self and achieved the way of *higher living*, true thinking becomes automatic and laborless. For us to continually embody absolute Love will surely cause loving thoughts to rise from their boundless depths and spring forth into a "well of living water." To live *consciously* as the spiritual Man instead of conforming ourselves with the human, or personal, will adjust all of our thinking automatically.

He who voluntarily parts company with that self who can feel hurt or offended, fearful or disturbed, unforgiving or unmerciful, has released himself likewise from these habits of thought which are contrary to the law of divine Love. Naturally the putting-off of the personal self includes the putting-off of his faulty human mind also—that mind of sick, sad, sinful thinking which is the mind of the personal man; and as we cease to function as this man, we gradually transcend the effects brought about by his mind. Moreover, as we lovingly and gladly express our true Self of love and peace, of joy and harmony, we simultaneously enter into "that mind which was also in Christ Jesus."

There is, indeed, a way of true living transcending the way of "taking thought. It is the practice of the presence of righteousness in you, the surrendering of that false estimate and activity of yourself as the sinful, mortal man for that spiritual Divinity which is waiting to be expressed in you. "When that which is perfect is come, then that which is in part shall be done away" (1 Cor. 13:10).

The rational human mind declares that "no man can be perfect," despite the fact that the Master's command is "Be ye therefore perfect, even as your Father which is in heaven is perfect" (Matt. 5:48). Fear, doubt, worry, anxiety, grief—all these emotions, since they are generated only in the mistaken human mind, belong to that soul acting in the position of the personal man; but divine Love embodied in oneself, and daily lived, will always meet and fill every human need.

While men *choose* to grope in darkness, they cannot receive the benefit of the revelations of the light. Let all turn toward the light who would receive it. Man should aspire to acquire freedom, harmony, and power by his willingness to serve the true Light in every action of his daily life; to live each moment as though divine Love were sharing his every thought and watching his every action, "for God is a discerner of the thoughts and intents of the heart" (Heb. 4:12).

We are told by the Master, Jesus, that "whatsoever ye shall ask in my name, I will do it." I recall how, at one time in my life, I pondered for many days and nights over the thought of prayer. It seemed to me that the perfect answer to our imperfect existence, here and now, would be to know how to pray aright. If, according to Jesus' words, everything good could be brought to pass *in his name*, then if we but clearly understood just what this promise meant, and applied it, we could set everything to rights in our world. So daily I asked God to teach me how to pray aright.

One night soon afterwards, I experienced a beautiful and extraordinary dream which gave me the answer to my intensely earnest desire. I seemed to be walking with my little daughter in a strange city. We were making our way down a street banked high with pure white snow. Everything, everywhere, seemed clothed all in white, even to the child who was dressed in a little white hat and coat. Soon we came to a group of children. I paused to speak to them, but as I turned to continue on, my own child had utterly vanished. Terrified, I called her name and looked about on all sides, but she was nowhere in sight. Then I seemed to feel how really hopeless it would be for me, on a strange street, amidst such huge banks of white snow, to ever find my white-clad little one. So in my dream, I stood distracted and filled with a terrible anguish.

A voice from somewhere about me seemed to say, "You will never see your child again." Now, in this deep agony of heart and great desperation of soul, suddenly the thought of prayer came strongly into my mind, and I remembered how I had been trying to learn the secret of true prayer. Oh, if only I had discovered the answer! thought I. Then, in my dream, I turned myself wholly to God in prayer. My mind seemed alive, brilliantly lighted with love and worship, but the prayer came from my lips as though someone else in me were saying the words through my mouth, so apart were they from the personal me.

Before telling you what these words were which contained the answer to my earnest questioning about prayer, bear in mind that the great need in my dream was to locate my lost child in that strange city. Naturally we would expect the prayer to be a petition to include the finding of the child in this situation. But quite to the contrary, the prayer had nothing to do with a lost child, nothing to do with snowy streets or a strange city. Here now is the prayer which sprang spontaneously from my lips, as in my fearful extremity I turned myself to God: "Dear God, open my eyes so that I may see my child lying in her crib by my bedside."

The Price of Glory

Gently my eyes opened, and there, directly in my vision, lay my little one, safe and sound, and fast asleep in her own comfortable crib.

What a great and marvelous lesson lies enfolded in this heaven-sent form of prayer. The great desire in my dream to locate my child in the strange city could not be granted for the simple reason that she was not there—she was somewhere else. How can we expect to find a thing except where it is located? Can we see the rising sun while we stand facing westward? Well, no more can we find our true selves while we stand looking into dreams and mirages for them! We must face the direction in which that for which we are hoping and praying may be expected to manifest!

Now, all the time that I thought my child was lost in the snow, she was tucked safely and soundly in her own little crib. Therefore, the true prayer which came straight from the God within me was not for the child's safety or for her deliverance, but that I myself might open my own eyes to see her where she really was! The instant that I awoke and saw her in her crib, a great thrill of joy filled me, not only that all was well but, more than this, that God had answered my heart's desire and taught me how to pray aright.

We are all so easily misled in our everyday experiences to believe that we should pray for deliverance from sickness, from sorrow, and from limitation. We are endlessly searching to find a way to be saved from our particular problems and delivered over to harmony and happiness. But trying to repair the dream of our material existence by ways and means of the human mind is vastly different from opening up our vision to behold the radiant never-changing glory and wholeness of our true Being, which is ours the instant we are willing to pay the price of Glory—*lay down that false personal self for it*.

We really never left our heavenly home, never actually wandered off to a far country; for after all, a dream-experience has no reality, has it? Therefore, if we would but clear our vision to receive of what we have already been given, to let the false personal self of our dream drop away from us as we *embody the perfect way of living*, how beautiful and all-satisfying our lives would be!

Do you recall how Mary Magdalene, heartbroken and sorely perplexed over the death of her Lord on the cross, went to the sepulcher, "and as she wept, she stooped down and looked into the tomb"? Now, how could she see him there when he was risen and was standing directly at her side that very instant? *When she looked up, then she saw him.*

Do you remember too the account given us about the servant of Elisha:

> Behold, an host compassed the city, both with horses and chariots ... Alas, my master! how shall we do? And Elisha prayed, and said, Lord, I pray thee, open his eyes, that he may see! And the Lord opened the eyes of the young man; and he saw; and behold, the mountain was full of horses and chariots of fire round about Elisha (2 Kings 6:15, 17).

We find Jesus himself ever *looking up* steadfastly to the Father within him. Where, then, shall we look for our ultimate salvation but to our own indwelling Christ, who will reveal the Father to us? Therefore, with clear understanding and a holy joy, let us keep our vision turned inward to him, our indwelling Christ, the one Mediator between God and man. Until we "lay down" our life as a separate, personal entity, we are unable to "take it up" as the true Character (Son) who is none other than the Father Himself, expressing (in infinite individualization) His own qualities and characteristics in Earth (out-pictured experience) as in heaven (inner consciousness).

Chapter XI

Practicing the Presence

There is a Wholeness we may partake of which is no part of this material existence but which can manifest to us as physical health and soundness. There is a Power we can individualize which is no part of any material forces but which can deliver to us a perfect way of escape from any evil thing. There is a Presence which is "not of earth, earthy" but is of the kingdom, heavenly, which can, here and now, surely lead us into that prosperity and success which we are all seeking.

As we are tested by life's experiences and proven worthy and as we increasingly "put on" the mind of Jesus Christ, thinking the things he thought, doing the things he did, and accomplishing in ourselves the things he commanded us to do, we will continually climb upward and advance onward, "until we all come unto a perfect man, unto the measure of the stature of the fulness of Christ."

To illustrate the practice of the Christ-Presence within and the surety of marvelous results received from this contact, let me describe a particular instance where a woman drew her supply directly from this Source, and another where a woman drew her happiness from this same Source. To cite the first instance:

A woman, living alone and self-supporting, lost her position in the business world, which was her only means of revenue. For two whole years, she made every effort to find work in the city in which she lived but with no success. The day finally came when she was about penniless, and on the following morning the little home which she had mortgaged was to be taken from her. This woman loved God with an enlightened faith and was greatly moved and troubled within her soul that she had not been able to contact this great presence of the All-Good.

As she sat in her room this last night, she was thinking of her great failure to *experience* this Good and of all that she would lose on the following day—her home, the place she so loved, with its beautiful green lawn and all its living, growing things. They would take her belongings too, all that she possessed of any value. She would lose her sanctuary, her place of refuge and shelter. Yes, all must go! And she had tried so hard, so very hard, to contact God and had failed in this also.

Then suddenly, in the midst of this sense of depression and despair, a beautiful revelation opened to her. They might take everything material, she thought, but they could not take her inner sanctuary, that "secret place" where she really lived "under the shadow of the Almighty"! Forgetting her trouble and grief, she thought now of that "house" described by Paul in the Bible: "For we know that if our earthly house were dissolved, we have a building of God, an house not made with hands, eternal in the heavens" (2 Cor. 5:1).

A gentle peace and a great gladness spread through her. To think that she had found something which they *could not take*. This eternal house—this, her place of refuge in the center of her Soul—they could not take this, *for this no man could touch*! So tonight she would worry no more about these other material things that she would lose in the morning; she would lie down and go to sleep in this *Something* within her which they could not take, this place of her real Being. And so, simply and lovingly, she surrendered herself wholly to God, her Creator.

When she awakened the next day, she still felt the thrill and the joy of the night before. What a peaceful night's rest she had had, free from all fear or worry, in this place she had newly discovered as being the only thing which belonged to her, the only thing which was hers *by divine right*.

With only lightness and buoyancy in her consciousness, she dressed and made herself ready for the men whom she knew would soon be at hand. A knock came upon the door. There stood, not the men whom she expected and had dreaded to see, but a young man politely touching his cap and handing her an envelope. It was a letter from a large and very important business firm in her city, asking her if she would come at once to them and accept the very excellent position they offered her.

So this woman who was to lose all her material possessions lost none of them. In locating her real and genuine Possession, nothing in her material living was disturbed. In contacting her spiritual Christ-Self, she found also her material good in this world, for ever the *form* of Good in this world is the outward expression of the Christ-consciousness within.

Now let me tell you how happiness too can be found by contacting this same Source of all-Good. Under very distressing circumstances, a woman lost her husband. She could not be consoled or quieted within her. It almost seemed to her that God had left her, although this woman too loved God devoutly. But with the loss of her husband, she felt also the loss of her spiritual joy, of peace, of companionship, and all that makes life lovely and complete.

Her grief was actuated not only by the separation from her husband but also by a feeling of remorse. Every day thoughts came to her about the things she should have done and had not done for him. Months and years passed, and while the cloud lifted from her to a great extent, the one thing she longed for, happiness in companionship, was missing. But she clung steadfastly to God and to that Light in her own soul.

One day, suddenly a revelation dawned in her consciousness. Was her happiness located in this particular person after all? Or was it to be found here and now, by contacting that great stream of happiness flowing for all from out of the Love-nature of God? New hope filled and uplifted her. But what about her remorse? It must go. She would leave that "far country" of sorrow and failure; she would confess her mistakes to God and then gladly and quickly take those steps demanded of her, straight back to her Father's house, where a new life and a new joy awaited her. *Thus did she surrender herself and her problem entirely to God, her real Being.*

In a few short weeks from that day, she came unexpectedly into the presence of a man she had never seen before. At once her heart stirred, and the still small voice spoke to her those words she had prepared herself to hear: *He is the one.* And in the heart of the man too there took place at the same time the same miracle of love. Within a few months they were married and found in each other the joy and companionship for which they had made themselves ready.

Dear friend, if it is health that you crave or release from social or financial worries, then begin at once to turn your heart and mind to completeness in God and all-sufficiency in Christ. For He made you, the real You, out of His own Love, Life, and Substance. He requires of you *utter dependence upon Him for all things*; not only for your spiritual growth in the development of your soul but for your physical health, your mental serenity, and your material supply.

He alone conceives the perfect eyes and clear sight; the perfect ears and acute hearing; the perfect mind and true thinking; the perfect organs and all their harmonious functions; the perfect world and all its spiritual activities. What a faint idea any of us has of the extent of the magnitude of beauty and glory of God's perfect creation—"above all that we ask or think."

So try to release yourself from your long unsuccessful dependence upon material ways and means of overcoming wrong conditions. Fix your heart and your mind upon God as your Creator and upon Christ as your physician and provider in every way and in everything. Let your faith and your trust in Him rise to new heights. Rejoice and give thanks that He is calling you now to believe in and accept His salvation from all your problems; for His promise is that if you but turn from the material world and its false inventions, the mortal self and its false beliefs, and *place your whole love, faith, and confidence in Him as your sure defense and deliverer*, you will reap the sure harvest of health and happiness, abundance and joy, right here on Earth today.

How could God send poverty or sickness to us, or any evil thing, when we are told, "Thou art of purer eyes than to behold evil, and canst not look upon iniquity"? (Hab. 1:13). If we do not obtain the right answers to our daily problems, it cannot be through some fault in Him. If we run away from trouble instead of casting out the "works of the flesh" right where we stand; if we refuse today to "put off the old man" and "put on the Christ," then naturally we must pay the penalty in unhappy consequences, such as lack and limitation, for this is the obvious fault of man himself, and he alone can set himself free from this state of bondage and limitation by applying the law of divine Love and Wisdom to his particular need.

You may have tried many ways of healing misery and pain, sadness and despair, in yourself and in others, but you have not tried *all* ways until you have used the purely spiritual way of practicing the presence of the Jesus-Identity in you and in the one needing help, steadfastly allowing this real Identity to rule supreme *in your thoughts and in your every action*, and seeing Father and Son as one!

No darkness can persist in the light; neither can evil withstand the power of "Christ in you," for ever he declareth, "All power is given unto me in heaven and in earth." The magic name, the magic power, the magic kingdom—all are within our very own Being, here and now. "With men (the personal) this is impossible; but with God all things are possible" (Matt. 19:26).

Beloved, let us begin to break in sunder the shackles of fear, doubt, and uncertainty and so prove our faith by our works. Who can conquer sin, sorrow, and all forms of suffering and limitation save the Spirit of Jesus Christ who is in us? This is why we must be ever *practicing His presence*, for it is the will of our Father that we come to ourselves and rise and return unto Him; that we leave "the far country" where "no man gave unto" us. Surely all compassion is expressed by Jesus Christ, who painted for us this word-picture which has no equal.

There are many today still depending on the personal man and the material world for help and salvation from evil; but those of us who have discovered what are the failings of the flesh and the shortcomings of the material world have heard the joyous word of the Christ-Spirit, who ever declares:

> *I* am the light of your world; in Me no darkness can exist. *I* am your Way; follow Me, and *I* will lead you into green pastures and beside the still waters.

> *I* am the Eternal One, the never-changing Power and the ultimate victory over all evil.
>
> *I* can transfigure and transform all things of your earthly experience through your transcending recognition of Me as your very life, mind, soul, and being, for "I am the vine, ye are the branches."
>
> Your life in Me shall bear rich fruitage, and in Me you shall ever progress to new levels of revelation, and new fields of service.

"Who 'convinceth me of sin' in my heavenly world of spiritual realities?" comes as a challenge from the all-victorious Christ in you and me:

> Come unto Me, and you will find freedom from your bondage, as in light you are free from darkness. Come unto Me, and you will find rest from the burdens and the cares of your material existence; for *I*, the inner Christ in you, and God, the Father of all, are one and the same Being.

So as we believe in and accept these "glad tidings," we find that we are not creatures of unyielding fate, but that we are the creators of our own destiny, and the yearnings, the "groanings," and the "travail" of the soul (which no doubt we all have felt at various times in our lives) all serve to bring us to that perfect place in the finished kingdom, prepared for us "from the foundation of the world"—that place which we shall inevitably find and fill.

But man must first feel this soul-hunger and acknowledge this soul-need! He must first realize the folly of his false sense of liberty and the deceits of his much illusioned life! The sun cannot shine into a room whose shutters are tightly closed; neither can the Son of righteousness shine into our hearts until they are opened wide and ready to admit Him.

The drama of the sacrifice on Calvary must be repeated in our own lives today. This means the crossing-out of the personality, with his sense of sin and shortcoming, from our thoughts and from our conduct, in order to prepare us for our resurrection from the dead, for Paul tells us that we are "dead in trespasses and sins" until "in Christ shall all be made alive."

Nor may we yield to the temptation to "come down from the cross" until "it is finished." Rather must we persevere in the spiritualization of our consciousness until all error ceases. Then the resurrecting power within ourselves will release us from the former self-imposed mortal state, and we shall partake of the experience of ascension, which shall be our final victory over evil. Jesus finished his work for us, but it is not finished in us until we too have triumphed over "the world, the flesh, and the devil."

The truth as taught by Jesus Christ is that a child can understand it, but the practice is the arduous work of a lifetime. Nevertheless, he said, "My yoke is easy and my burden is light" when compared with "the wages of sin" and the "husks which the swine did eat" of the prodigal personality.

"Ye believe in God, believe also in me," says the Jesus Christ within you, for "He that hath the Son hath the Father also." Since the personality of the best of us is liable to express imperfection at any time, this very day is none too soon to resolve to separate ourselves from the personal man, to be "in the world but not of it," and to unify ourselves only with the immortal qualities of the ever-living Christ of us.

Jeremiah perfectly understood the frailties of the personal man when he cried, "O Lord, I know that the way of man is not in himself: it is not in man that walketh to direct his steps" (Jer. 10:23). How often we find Paul comparing the spiritual Man with his human shadow. In speaking of his own "hope of glory," he writes: "Though the outward man perish, yet the inward man is renewed day by day; not that we would be unclothed, but clothed upon, that mortality might be swallowed up of life" (2 Cor. 4:16; 5:4).

It is written that at the name of Jesus everything in heaven and Earth shall bow. Truly, if this name be in our hearts, his power shall be in our lives. Jesus is Health *expressed*; Jesus is Love *represented*; Jesus is Power *manifested*. Thus, you and I, and everyone, are to accept and "put on" the Lord-Self, the Jesus-Identity, for it is written:

> I, Jesus, am the bright Morning Star. I (Jesus) am Alpha and Omega, the beginning and the end, the first and the last ... I (Jesus) am the door of the sheep. Verily, verily, I say unto you, he that entereth not by the door into the sheepfold, but climbeth up some other way, the same is a thief and a robber ... by me if any man enter in, he shall be saved, and shall go in and out, and find pasture ... Behold, I come quickly; and my reward is with me.

Therefore, the admonition is given us again and again to *believe* and to *receive*. If we do not believe in Him as the *inner Reality* and *Identity* of us each, then we are not in a position to *receive* Him and *experience* Him in our outer lives and our contacts with the world. If we do not receive a proffered gift, of what advantage is it to have seen it? So, dear ones, put aside your personal ego and your selfish pride, for they that "hear the word, and receive it ... bring forth fruit, some thirtyfold, some sixty and some an hundred."

Do you recall the healing of the blind Bartimaeus, who cried out to Jesus to save him? The very first thing this man did, upon being told that Jesus had sent for him, was to "cast away his garments," allowing nothing to impede his response. It was as if a great insight simultaneously arose within him, for when Jesus asked, "What wilt thou that I do unto thee?" the blind man gave the astonishingly significant request, "Lord, that I might receive my sight" (Mark 10:51).

How many of us are watchful enough and sufficiently awake mentally to realize the supreme importance of attaining that consciousness which can receive the good that "God hath prepared for those that love him"? For no matter how much is prepared, if we do not receive it, it avails us nothing.

So, dear one, do not bar your heart against the tender, loving provision of God, but open it wide to receive to yourself the gifts which He, in His all-knowing wisdom and all-loving care, has made ready for you. Lay aside now your superimposed personality, with its vanity and self-importance, and like the blind Bartimaeus, who "immediately received his sight," you too will immediately receive the particular good which is present right now where you stand and which awaits only your loving acceptance of it to bless and prosper you.

Jesus became the embodiment of divine Love; he lived perfection and demonstrated eternal Life. And we must become at one with him if we expect to share in his power and glory. To "put on" his goodness, we are required to give up everything which is unlike goodness; for in so doing, we become one with him who is our true Identity, and then "we shall be like him, for we shall see him as he is."

Therefore, let no one delude himself with the notion that beautiful ideas and right words alone can save him, for only when these are *lived* and *expressed* in our world of every day can our lives show forth His praise. "That men may see your good works, and glorify (not you but) your Father which is in heaven."

The religion of Jesus Christ is one of action and expression, aiming to put an end to sin in thought, word, and deed. Verily, the path of return is so straight and narrow that he who would walk in it securely can take with him no selfish personal desires or unloving thoughts whatsoever as his companions.

The whole value of Jesus' life and teaching for us is that we might live as he lived; that we might love as he loved; that we might overcome "the world, the flesh, and the devil" as he did. But how could we do such difficult things except by becoming at one with his Spirit, his nature, and his character? *Only by unifying our minds and our hearts with him* can we surely rise to the same heights of spiritual achievement as he promised us we could do.

To help us practice the presence of Jesus Christ within us, we can keep before us such aspirations as these:

> I recognize the indwelling Christ in me as the real and true of me, and with all my heart and soul and being I desire to manifest and to express in my disposition and conduct only this Christ-Being.
>
> From this disposition, I am conscious of the Christ in me, and I see this same Christ in others. I know that the Christ knoweth no evil, but understandeth always the unreality of evil appearances and dissolves them by and with His own presence.
>
> I bring my heart to this Christ, asking Him to keep me free from evil thinking and evil doing, and to hold me perfect in Himself always. I recognize my good, which He has already given to me, and here and now I accept it and rejoice in it, for in this way only am I accepting Jesus Christ and unifying myself with Him— my real Being.

Verily, verily, to open the door of consciousness to *receive* and then *put into practice* the Jesus Christ Presence as here and now in us and among us places us in direct contact with the Christ-Power awaiting individualization. Jesus exemplified for us how to confidently claim the truth of our Being; how to hold steadfastly to our highest vision of Reality; and how to uncompromisingly love and serve our Father which art in heaven within us. "If ye shall ask anything in my name, I will do it."

> And I will take sickness away from the midst of thee (Exod. 23:25).

Accepting his Identity as that of free Spirit, always one with the highest good, man will go forward and upward, out from the partial and limited into the complete and perfect; from the seeing "as in a glass, darkly," to the viewing "face to face." For how little can any of us know, at present, of the great wealth of Glory which lies enfolded in our acceptance of our true Identity, Jesus Christ, except as "God hath revealed it unto us by his Spirit."

Chapter XII

Transcendent Love

The truth taught by Jesus Christ deals directly with man's heart. "The Lord seeth not as man seeth; for man looketh on the outward appearance, but the Lord looketh on the heart" (1 Sam. 16:7).

Only as man's heart opens to his Christ-Self can he be reborn and receive his true inheritance of present participation in the Life everlasting. As the heart expands and softens with love, the mind is spontaneously freed from its egotism, its hatred, revenge, unforgiveness, passion, selfishness, evil-thinking, and evil-speaking. And nothing short of this all-embracing love in the heart will ever cause a man to completely renounce the personal self!

> Therefore if thou bring thy gift to the altar, and there rememberest that thy brother hath ought against thee; leave there thy gift before the altar, and go thy way; first be reconciled to thy brother, and then come and offer thy gift ... Verily, I say unto thee, Thou shalt by no means come out thence, till thou hast paid the uttermost farthing (Matt. 5:23-24, 26).

Through this second birth, man learns to transcend the experiences of the material world, wherein the laws of man control him, and finds his place in that realm, here on Earth, wherein the law of divine Love is all-sufficient for him. Thus, if one would consciously become the Son of God and so partake of this experience of everlasting Good, he must lay aside the life of the personal man with its selfish objectives and take up the life of the Christ in him, whose law is written on the tablets of the heart.

To experience this rebirth is to be physically and materially benefited as well, for "the love of Christ constraineth us" and moves the heart to express gentleness, tenderness, compassion, mercy, understanding, and forgiveness, which bring in their own blessed harvest. This holy glow in the heart not only saves us from ignorance and its sad consequences but has power to lift us into a new life-expression here and now, for it transforms the whole character of man—mentally, physically, and emotionally. The ecstasy of divine Love in a man should not be translated as mere personal emotion but as the steady orientation of the soul to that which is eternal—its own God-Being.

"The time cometh, and now is" when the intellectual achievements of the mind must be balanced by the heart's spiritual understanding of the Christ. Aspiration, inspiration, consecration, and revelation are acquirements pertaining to the heart, the Love-nature of man. Nothing short of man's absolute willingness to obey the will of God will ever be the means of the complete surrender of his vain opinions, his lust for personal power, his hypocrisies, and his colossal selfishness.

When one wishes to serve truly the Divine in him, his eyes must ever be on the all-loving Jesus-way of thinking and living. He is then in bondage to no man. He "shall see God" in all, for he is pure of heart. He has nothing of himself to conceal or to defend; he has no personal interests to guard or protect. He enjoys the freedom of the Truth.

Yes, our lives must ever be in demonstration of the Truth we profess. When bitter feelings leave the heart, the consequent hard thoughts and harsh words go as well. Our transcendent Christ and our personal consciousness cannot dwell together, but if we do not act out our guidance when we come to feel the pressure of this divine Christ-life upon us, then it will prove of no real advantage, for it will fade out and leave us. "My spirit shall not always strive with man" (Gen. 6:3).

The endeavor to practice absolute love as Jesus did is bound to aid us in embodying his qualities of goodness, purity, mercy, and forgiveness. Loving as Jesus loved will help us to live as Jesus lived, and living as Jesus lived will ultimately deliver us from the age-long dream of mortality. We are all one in Him, but just as each of us, in this world, must individually eat and drink in order to be nourished, so in our higher walk of life, we are each required to partake of Him, "the living bread which came down out of heaven," for "if any man eat of this bread, he shall live forever."

Do you now see, dear ones, that to bring peace and the all-good to man while he still remains in his false belief of life is not in accord with God's plan for his salvation? While in the material consciousness, man will never find a way of permanently healing sickness and sorrow and eradicating them forever from the Earth; for the "healing of the nations," the bringing of the eternal Wholeness to man while he chooses to remain in the "far country" is impossible, and it is not the Father's purpose for the world's redemption.

The mere mental concept of yourself as the Son of God, and thus as wise, successful, or virtuous, will never be the means of your complete deliverance from want, ignorance, or sin. But the joyous yielding of yourself wholly to the sustaining, victorious Christ in you and the acceptance of His manifold goodness to you, with all the strength and ardor of your whole Being, will be the way to experience that Christ-Consciousness which you have so long desired.

So give up your confidence in personal speculations and inventions, for as a man translates himself from the lower to the higher consciousness, he finds the Father ever waiting to reinstate him and to command:

> Bring forth the best robe, and put it on him; and put a ring on his hand, and shoes on his feet; and bring hither the fatted calf, and kill it ... for this my son was dead, and is alive again; he was lost, and is found (Luke 15:22-24).

Such is the nature of divine Love, which gives for our hunger Its sustenance; for our repentance, Its cancellation; and for our tears and griefs, Its own eternal gladness.

The younger son typifies the *teachable* heart of man, while the elder manifests unforgiveness, resentment, jealousy, self-pity, and typifies the *personal mind* of man. This mind is hard and calculating; it would reach its own decisions and then selfishly and heartlessly act upon them, while the regenerate heart, though capable of making mistakes too, can be easily purified and redeemed by Love and has fully humbled itself in order to receive of its desired inheritance.

Although the Father had said to the elder son, "All that I have is thine," that mind could not have received of this good, else he would not have desired to deprive his brother from sharing in it. His portion of goods had not blessed him, for he had not *received* it unto himself nor made himself at one with it. Watch therefore, beloved, that you do not shut God from your heart even while with your mind you claim relationship to Him; rather, be so deeply in love with God that with both your heart and your mind you will receive Him unto yourself.

It is often asked, "How can I cultivate love for God? How can I feel the presence of the Christ?" By lovingly recognizing His beauty in all His creation and by knowing that "for thy pleasure they were and are created."

For is there anyone who does not love Beauty revealed in the glowing stars, the tinted skies, the singing birds, the blooming flowers? If you love all these, you are loving God, for He is not apart from any of His works.

Why, you cannot raise your eyes without coming in contact with His presence! How can you drink in the beauty of the world about you, how can you partake of the ever-developing possibilities of your own evolving life, without feeling that *it is all from Him*? Moreover, whenever you do kindly deeds, think generous thoughts, or express His loving nature in you, you are at one with Him, whether consciously or not. For Love is but another name for God. Harmony, joy, kindness, peace—these are all qualities of His Being. So let your life continue to praise Him, "for herein is your Father glorified, that ye bear much fruit," and soon you will more and more feel His presence with you.

One can cultivate his mind by higher ways of thinking; how much more should he attune his heart to more abundant ways of loving! Learn to love your work and your play. Try to love the life of every day, no matter how difficult that may seem, for it is testing you to think and feel about it the way you should. Have that faith in God which looks to Him alone as the Source of your health, your happiness, your prosperity, and your success. Such absolute surrender of yourself and all your affairs to God will surely prepare your heart to find these blessings in Him and to feel that His love is the greatest thing in all the world to you.

> I counsel thee to buy of me gold tried in the fire, that thou mayest be rich: and white raiment, that thou mayest be clothed, and that the shame of thy nakedness do not appear (Rev. 3:18).
>
> What are these which are arrayed in white robes and whence came they? These are they which came out of great tribulation, and have washed their robes, and

made them white in the blood of the Lamb (Rev 7:13-14).

For the Lamb which is in the midst of the throne shall feed them, and shall lead them unto living fountains of waters; and God shall wipe away all tears from their eyes (Rev. 7:17).

Many write to me asking how they may gain that "divine spark" which will set their souls aflame and bring them into the presence of God and His eternal harmonies. The answer is: *through the complete and loving surrender of yourself to God.* Since He is Love, then how should we hope to find Him, see Him, feel Him, know Him, receive Him, except through our absolute surrender to Him? No other way of approach, no other manner of thinking, living, or doing, will ever bring you into His presence so swiftly, so laborlessly, so all-compellingly as your complete yielding to Him—willing, all-surrendering, and boundless.

In your home and daily environment is the place where you must begin to open your heart and soul to His presence, for remember, "Charity (love) begins at home." So do not think to make a beginning from any other point, *for the place whereon you stand is the place where you must begin to love.* Express it spontaneously to those near and dear to you and do not ask them to take it for granted; for in order for love to be kept alive in your heart, it must be expressed by tender words and by considerate actions.

You may be asking, "How shall I begin?" Your pure desire is your beginning. Then turn yourself to God and ask Him to open your heart, to give it of His life by causing it to love. For what right have we to enjoy the wonders and beauties of this Earth, or why should we dare hope to make a success of our efforts to obtain prosperity, health, peace, or any worthwhile thing, unless we are in love with God, the Creator of all these things, and living in obedience to His will for us?

Without love in his heart, man is doomed to failure. Asleep in self, deafened and blinded by hypocrisies, indifference, or procrastination, he is but postponing this only way of ever attaining that quality of life which is worthwhile—that quality which is Love transcendent.

Why not begin today to tear down the "middle wall" between you and your good, your happiness, your health, your peace, and your prosperity? Only by being Love can you gain the fruits of the kingdom of heaven. Think of it! Even though you might fulfill every requirement or demand made upon you—though you might preach the gospel from the pulpit, practice the spiritual method of healing the sick, or win applause through your eloquence and cultured language and rise to the height of personal success and happiness—it will in the end profit you nothing if you have not done all in Love!

"Be not deceived; God is not mocked!" His eternal law of Love remains ever the only path of return to Him and His gifts. Verily, the stature of the perfect Man is measured by his Love manifestation, and without the fulfillment of this love in our hearts and its embodiment in our lives, we are but "as sounding brass and tinkling cymbals"—in other words, our lives will go out as wordless sounds die on the air.

The hunger in the heart for God will continue despite the most intensive training which may be applied to the mind. And it is this *hungering and thirsting after righteousness*, and for the true identification, which will bring the aspirant that influx of intuitive Light which transfigures his life and his world with its power to transform, for "as many as received him, to them gave he power to become the sons of God."

The search for Self-perfection does not imply that perfection pertaining to the lower self; it means that each of us must discover and make manifest our perfection in Him, the one true Self, who is our Savior (Jesus) Christ. This is the spiritual Man who, when generally accepted as humanity's genuine Being, will bring the promised Millennium into the experience of the world to put an end to all sin and death. "And the glory of the Lord shall be revealed, and all flesh shall see it together" (Isa. 40:5).

The specific work of each of us is to be this Man and become at one with him in our minds, in our hearts, and in our everyday experiences, thus hastening the coming of His radiance into manifestation. Every book and every teacher, every enlightened soul who has pointed out the truth of the indwelling Christ and His perfect kingdom within us and has striven to live and embody the beauty of the inner life of the soul, has blessed not only himself but the whole world and advanced it that much nearer to the goal of the Millennium.

A tremendously important point for us to always bear in mind is this: the *unreal* and *temporal* nature of sin, sickness, mortal existence, and all evil whatsoever. It is not the purpose of this book to give in detail an explanation of this advanced and enlightened perception; however, as one clarifies his consciousness and advances steadily in his progress toward the truth of Life, he is bound to come face to face with the fact that as the Christ-Consciousness is the only real and true one for us to recognize and acquire, and as the kingdom of heaven is always at hand and within us, evil must be a temporal and unreal state of mind induced by ignorance and sin.

"We all (as individuals), with open face (receptive vision) beholding as in a glass (crystal clearness) the glory of the Lord (the one perfect Christ-Self of us all), are changed into the same image from glory to glory, even as by the Spirit of the Lord" (2 Cor. 3:18). "As we have borne the image of the earthy (the mortal human personality), we shall also bear the image of the heavenly (the spiritual and the divine Man)" (1 Cor. 15:49). "There is one body, and one Spirit, even as ye are called in one hope of your calling; one Lord, one faith, one baptism; one God and Father of all, who is above all, and through all, and in you all" (Eph. 4:4-6).

Watch! We are standing in the midst of our own consciousness, judging ourselves daily, hourly; for our external world but reflects our inner state of consciousness. We see that the Christ is none other than the Creator made manifest in us; that "God the Father" *(Spirit)*, "God the Son" *(Jesus Christ)*, and "God the Holy Ghost" *(Illumination)* are one Being—infinite, complete, indivisible.

> And there shall be no more curse; but the throne of God and of the Lamb shall be in it. And they shall see his face; and his name shall be in their foreheads (Rev. 22:3-4).
> Blessed are they that do his commandments, that they may have right to the tree of life, and may enter in through the gates into the city (Rev. 22:14).
> And the Spirit and the bride say, Come. And let him that is athirst come. And whosoever will, let him take the water of life freely (Rev 22:17).

As we surrender ourselves wholly to our God and to the one "altogether lovely" Jesus Christ-Reality of us all, we shall transcend all the discordant conditions of our personal experiences, together with all their limitation, and we shall know that we are hereby paying the price of Glory, for we shall find ourselves in a New Day—the Day of perpetual blessedness, the Day of transcendent Love.

About the Author

Lillian DeWaters was born in 1883 and lived in Stamford Connecticut. She grew up with a Christian Science background and in her early teens began to study metaphysics and on that same day to seriously study the Bible. "It was from the Bible that I learned to turn from all else to God direct ... What stood out to me above all else was the fact presented, that when they turned to God they received Light and Revelation; they walked and talked with God, and they found peace and freedom."

She published several books while actively within the Christian Science organization. Then in 1924, she had an awakening experience, when it was as though a veil was parted and Truth was revealed to her. From that point, she began to receive numerous unfoldments and became a prolific writer.

She created her own publishing company and published over 30 books in 15 languages. She was a well-known teacher who taught regularly at the Waldorf Astoria in New York and was sought after as a spiritual healer.

Each of her books was written based on direct unfoldments of Absolute Truth that serious students will immediately recognize and treasure.

www.ingramcontent.com/pod-product-compliance
Lightning Source LLC
Chambersburg PA
CBHW030002050426
42451CB00006B/86